Serve

Stop taking and start giving, your key to sustainable and ethical marketing success

Mitchel White

ISBN: 9781677107032

Imprint: Independently published

Serve

Mitchel White founded his branding and marketing agency Reward in Manchester at the age of 21. Since then he has worked with brands across B2B and B2C sectors, including Europe's leading online destination for fashion Zalando, multi million pound manufacturing brands and exciting ecommerce startups. His work has been featured on Forbes, B2B Marketing and IndieHackers.

With a focus on sustainability and ethical marketing he writes regularly about the challenges he has faced in business and his personal life to help others achieve their dreams and goals.

Find out more at mitchelwhite.com and rewardagency.co.uk

Contents

Author's Note

Marketing has been misunderstood for as long as I can remember, granted at the time of writing I've only been on the planet for 26 years but whoever you speak to has a different understanding of what marketing is. Marketing Managers will tell you it's about conversions and Joe on the street might tell you it's TV advertising.

Why is marketing misunderstood?

Simply because it's overly complicated and has evolved over time to incorporate far too many things. We seem to have lost touch with the fact that marketing is about people. If we get back to the basics of why we market - it's to make a change. Whether it's a change in a person's lifestyle, choices, wealth, business success or their fitness. All marketing at some point brings about a change in someone's state, yet so many marketing professionals and entrepreneurs are bringing about negative change. Marketing should be using this power for good, not to generate bigger profits for unethical brands but to have a positive impact on people. Marketers and entrepreneurs need to serve their audience.

This book is for the forward thinking people who want to use their unique position and skills to bring about positive change, whether that's by reducing waste, by improving health, or in any other way that benefits people and the planet.

Success isn't limited

A common misconception in marketing and business is that someone has to lose for us to win. The truth is there's enough success to go around. You just need to find where yours is going to come from. Don't get jealous or downhearted when someone else achieves something, it proves what you want can be achieved. You just need to find your space to thrive. The purpose of this book is to give you a process to build an impactful brand you and your customers love.

The book is split into 3 sections, helping you to **Define** your audience, **Communicate** with them effectively and **Amplify** the power of that message with ethical marketing.

Enjoy building your brand!

For more information on the ideas in this book please visit mitchelwhite.com or rewardagency.co.uk

Section 1: Define
Find yourself and the people who care
Planning, research, branding

Resource: The Define Tree

Use The Define Tree to build a seven tier tree supported at the base by the most important question you need to ask yourself as a brand. Why do we exist? Once you've read this section, you should have a better understanding of each of the tiers. Come back to this resource and fill out each one to help you build a strong, impactful brand ready to serve people who care.

Our aim

What do we do?

How do we act?

What are our values?

What makes us unique?

Who do we serve?

Why do we exist?

CHAPTER 1
Too many businesses

Most industries are now flooded with competition.

The barriers to entry in most markets are at an all time low. To set up an ecommerce store all you need to do is set up a store on Shopify, create social profiles and market it to death. To set up a social media marketing agency you don't need any qualifications - just a laptop and results from previous social media campaigns.

Or so people think.

The truth is the lack of barriers to entry can actually be a bad thing. There are now far too many businesses competing for too few customers. With the entry of hundreds of startups to most industries every year, but the same number of customers usually existing in most established markets, it just makes it harder for everyone to compete in the category.

The first rule of economics - supply and demand - teaches us that when supply outstrips demand prices within an industry fall. In simplistic terms, more competition = lower prices.

But what about the few businesses at the top? The few guys at the top who still seem to do well, picking up the majority of business whilst the rest struggle, fighting each other with discounting, advertising and the latest shiny marketing tactic.

They're still fighting for business but they're sailing above the rest. Why? Because they have set themselves apart from the rest of the industry. Either with reputation, a USP, branding or being the only option in a customer's mind.

We live in uncertain times with big changes in spending habits, globalisation and demographic shifts.

Globalisation means national businesses are now competing internationally. A developer in London is competing with a developer in Mumbai. A marketer in Manchester is competing for business with their counterparts in Poland. Globalisation is an amazing thing. It's allowed us the opportunity to network with the world, to make friends across the globe and visit stunning countries.

But with it comes its own challenges and marketers must adapt to the effect globalisation has had on prices and industry. You can no longer sit back and compete locally - marketers and brands need to think beyond their own location and find their place in the new world.

Baby Boomers

What have Baby Boomers (the generation of people born between 1946 and 1964) got to do with marketing?

Most marketing decisions are made because of someone's stage in life or current situation. Someone who has just moved into a new home might be in the market for furniture, someone who has just got engaged might be looking at wedding venues, someone who just had a baby will probably be searching for baby products.

When there are a large concentration of people within a certain demographic like Baby Boomers or Millennials - they tend to create economic booms. In America, 76 million babies were born between 1946 and 1964. 45% of those Baby Boomers bought their homes between the ages of 25 and 34 - meaning over 34 million Baby Boomers bought a new home over a 9 year period. With so many people making one of the biggest purchases they had made to date, all of these people moved through traditional marketers buying funnels at the same time creating new industries and huge wealth for brands who catered to their changing needs.

We can follow similar economic booms through by tracking the ages of Baby Boomers. Car purchases, medical insurance and holiday destinations all correlate to where the mass of Baby Boomers were in their life cycle.

As Baby Boomers have gotten older we've seen the rise of private companies providing residential homes for the elderly and the number of cruises increase. Whole industries have been created to cater to the changing demographics in developed countries.

Baby Boomers are a generation who have enjoyed a long period of wealth. But they haven't always had it easy, they were the first to be exposed to TV advertising - for the first time they had a glimpse of what the wealthiest were getting up to. They saw celebrity endorsements and the latest gadget for the kitchen.

They were perhaps the first aspirational demographic, striving for more and sometimes being disappointed when their reality didn't match that of others.

Something a lot of Millenials can relate to.

Millennials become the biggest adult generation

In 2019, Millennials have overtaken Baby Boomers as the single largest adult generation in developed countries like the US and UK.

What does this mean for marketing?

As Millennials (the generation of people born between 1981 and 1996) reach their prime working and spending years, their impact on the economy is going to be huge. Changes in the affordability of housing is a big issue with more people turning away from home ownership and choose renting.

Millennials are also more likely to be single and without children than Baby Boomers which alters conventional thinking around the age at which traditional purchases are made. Car ownership among the younger generation is falling and is expected to have peaked in the 2000s.

All of these factors have resulted in impacts across various markets. Housing, car buying and retail have been particularly affected by changing demographics as Millennial spending and behavioural habits shake things up.

Changing demographics & priorities

Purpose and identity are two words commonly used by people who fall into the Millennial category. The need to identify with a purpose and to carve your own identity has become a huge part of modern day culture.

We have a different set of priorities to previous generations.

You not only strive for more for yourself but for those you care about and often the planet. Our purpose is driven by more than ourselves and we're often seen as the fluffy generation because of our need for fulfillment.

But is that such a bad thing? Is it bad to want to improve the lives of others and the planet?

Brands that heed this message are thriving and building communities of people who are engaged and mobilised to be a part of the brand's purpose.

Why do businesses exist?

Why do businesses exist in the first place? The obvious thing that springs to mind is to create wealth for the person who set the business up.

But beyond that businesses exist to:

- Create employment and nurture talent

- Contribute to the economy through taxation

- Drive innovation with new products and services

But really when it comes down to it most people are in business because they don't want to work 9-5 for someone else. They want to create their own future and make a bit of money doing it instead.

So what's the point of your business existing?

Beyond making money, why does your business exist?

What's the point?

If you're just here to make a bit of money you're more than likely not going to last long in the competitive landscape of modern business and startups.

Eight in ten companies fail within their first year.

There are lots of reasons why businesses fail, but these three are perhaps some of the most important reasons:

- They don't solve a real problem

- They run out of money

- There is no differentiation i.e. they're the same as everyone else

The running out of money issue is pretty obvious. If your outgoings are higher than your income for a sustained period, you're going to run into cash flow problems and your business will fail. The other two reasons are perhaps a little more complicated. The problem of no differentiation stems from a bigger problem. There are too many players in most sectors. The big boys in each sector account for the majority of revenue and everyone else is fighting for the leftovers.

If you're not in an industry it's easy to look in and see the success stories written in the news and on social media. But what you don't see is the rest of the market struggling to make any money or headway.

Before you enter into an already saturated market, think carefully and ask yourself "do we really need someone else in this space?"

If the answer is yes, ask yourself "What's the point?"

Hopefully this will get you thinking about the real reasons you want to get into business in that particular market.

It should come down to there being a problem you have noticed that you can solve better than anyone else is currently. One where you can really add value to a customer's life and do it better than anyone else already in the market.

Going beyond product market fit

So you've identified your market and the problem you want to solve.

When you've proven that a customer will pay you to solve a specific problem you've found something called your "product market fit."

Marc Andreessen, the co-founder of venture capital firm Andreessen Horowitz, defined the term product market fit as *"being in a good market with a product that can satisfy that market."*

Lots of business and startup blogs talk about finding your product market fit but what they don't talk about is the fact that a lot of founders lose sight of why they started their business in the first place.

When you're bogged down in developing a product or growing a business it's easy to forget that problem, so when you're building your business constantly ask "What's the point?"

It will keep you aligned with the problem you're trying to solve and remind you why you developed the idea in the first place.

Going beyond profit

One way to really get yourself motivated and finally answer the "What's the point?" question is to have a purpose beyond profit in your organisation.

The likes of glasses retailer Warby Parker and shoe brand TOMS are prime examples of brands thriving with social change at their core.

Often founders and management teams run out of steam and energy when they're starting out by trying to grow with overworked teams who barely make it to the end of the week without burning out.

If you have a purpose beyond profit, the chances of you getting demotivated are a lot lower – because you're working towards something you're truly passionate about.

It's your responsibility to carry on ploughing forward, because you are the person put on this planet to make the change you're pushing for.

Saving the planet, helping reduce poverty or making lives better is a much bigger motivator than your P&L sheet.

Constantly ask yourself "What's the point?" Never ask it in a negative way but in a challenging way to keep you aligned with your goals and ambitions.

CHAPTER 2
Take, take, take

If we're honest, marketing right now is shocking. We're constantly bombarded with online and offline advertisements on Facebook, in service station toilets, on our TVs, on YouTube and on huge billboards causing enormous light pollution.

Our attention is being stolen and our days interrupted by poorly targeted and badly written adverts passed off as marketing.

If you're a marketer, you'll know why it is. You're measured on metrics - how many impressions, how many click throughs and how many sales have come from the ads.

Now I'm not saying you don't need metrics or adverts (more on the alternative in later chapters). But we do need to look at the take, take, take culture that has existed in marketing and business for far too long.

Getting back to marketing basics

It's no wonder marketing has gotten so confused. When you search "what is marketing?" on Google you're greeted with this definition -

"the action or business of promoting and selling products or services, including market research and advertising"

This is where it all goes wrong for me. Selling and marketing are two completely different things Now they should be aligned and there needs to be a closer relationship between sales and marketing, but marketing isn't there purely for sales and shouldn't be measured in terms of quick sales results.

The CIM (Chartered Institute of Marketing) defines marketing as *"the management process responsible for identifying, anticipating and satisfying customer requirements profitably."*

This to me is a better definition. Identifying, anticipating and satisfying customer requirements should be the foundation of any successful marketing strategy. If you wanted to go one step further, you could add in "to exceed customer requirements."

Most marketers aren't marketing

Most organisations are starting their marketing planning from an organisational perspective. Yes, marketing needs to deliver results and will contribute to the sustained success of a brand, but the real starting point of any marketing activity should be identifying, anticipating and satisfying customer needs.

The anticipating part here is really important. Successful organisations are the best in their industries at anticipating needs. They're ahead of the competition because they're thinking ahead. What will be the next innovation within our organisation to have a positive effect on our customers' lives? What can be done differently internally to make the customer experience better?

These are all questions forward thinking brands should be asking themselves each and every day. In reality though, most marketers are trying to improve their email open rates, social media engagement figures and conversion rates. While these are all important metrics to track, they shouldn't be the driving force behind your marketing.

The driving force behind your marketing should be an unwavered focus on making customers' lives that little bit better by existing.

Before jumping into taking money from customers or spending time trying to improve marketing tactic performance, look at the bigger picture. What value am I adding to this person's life? If you're not adding any maybe it's time to consider trying to drive change in your existing organisation. If others are reluctant to move forward with you, maybe it's time for a change in job or to go it alone.

People don't trust advertising and marketing

In a 2015 study of Americans by research company IpsosOTX on the integrity of the marketing industry only 4% of those surveyed thought the marketing and advertising industry acted with integrity. Trust in marketing was below financial institutions, newspapers and even Congress!

What's more, 96% of those surveyed didn't trust the advertising and marketing messages they see.

That's huge! People trust the word of a stranger for a recommendation and the word of the government (let's not even go there) over an organisation's own advertising. That's what years of false promises and underdelivering does for you.

For years, marketers have taken consumers' money with little thought for whether their product is the right fit for that consumer and how it might affect their lives now and in the future.

Using more tools to take time from audiences

If you're old enough to remember the days before dial up, you'll remember the amount of leaflets you got through the door, the flashy TV adverts and full page newspaper ads. The number of ways to get in front of an audience was limited. Nowadays, the number of marketing tools at our fingertips is mindblowing. From Instagram to Google, email to Facebook Messenger, the ways we can get in front of people as marketers is amazing.

But scary.

We can interrupt someone's day with an email or message direct to their Facebook account within seconds of us typing it. With chatbots and automated messaging - we can schedule ahead for the optimum sending time when a person is most likely to be using a platform. Whilst this is a huge benefit to marketers, is it really that great for consumers?

As new platforms like Tik Tok storm the App Store and the number of ways to reach customers increases, the problem of always being switched on and open to marketing messages is only going to get bigger.

Information overload

We live in a burnout culture. One in four people in the UK will experience a mental health problem each year and the way we live is having an impact on the problem. We're constantly switched on and open to information.

Our ancient brains haven't changed much in 30,000 years but our surroundings and lifestyles have. We're all guilty of using our phones too much, of spending too much time in front of a screen, of not taking enough breaks during the day, of not taking enough time to recover. It's all impacting our health and marketers are contributing to the problem.

In the 70s the average consumer would see around 500 adverts a day. At the time of writing we potentially now see over 5,000 ads a day. Add that to longer working hours and more stressful jobs - it's no wonder we're living in a burnout culture.

What's the alternative?

The tide is turning and more people than ever are being more frugal with their spending and how they spend their time. Actively trying to reduce their screen time and exposure to information.

Millions of people globally are using ad blocking technology and we're becoming better over time at tuning out from marketing messages with our BS detectors performing better than ever.

So what's the alternative? How can we move away from the take, take, take culture of marketing and move towards a more customer friendly version of marketing? One focused on delivering real value to our audience.

Serve.

It's that simple. Serve your audience.

Provide value. Real value - not stuff they don't want or need. Build a community of like minded people who align with your unique values and beliefs and create a better world for them. People need you to deliver the change they want, they want you to succeed. In return they give you their attention, their trust and their money. But it's not a transactional relationship. It's something much deeper and long lasting. Bringing your organisation sustainable, long term growth and success.

Authenticity

In a world of influencers it's hard to tell what's authentic and what isn't. We're all constantly comparing ourselves to others. We try to replicate the latest hairstyles, makeup looks and outfits from our favourite Instagram personality.

When it comes to brands, it's no different. The latest apparel company is trying to be GymShark. The latest tech startup is trying to be the next Uber. The latest fashion brand is trying to be Boohoo.

True authenticity is difficult to come by but it represents a big opportunity for your business. In their 2017 Consumer Content Report Stackla found 86% of consumers say authenticity is a key differentiator that leads to a purchasing decision and 94% of consumers say they would remain loyal to a brand that provides complete transparency.

Being authentic is pretty straightforward.

Decide what you stand for, be open about what you stand for and stick by it. Don't be fickle and move onto the latest value trend. Stick to your guns and be a truly authentic brand. Research proves that being authentic attracts and retains valuable customers.

Modern consumers demand transparency. It's not a 'nice to have,' it's a must have in today's business environment. Brands need to share more information than ever before, from transparency on materials used in products to website pages.

Consumers now have access to more information than ever and they're using it. A quick search shows us everything we need to know about brands – whether it's to verify product claims or see past stories about the business.

Consistency

Marketers have no loyalty to their audience.

Brands that fail are those who forget who their audience is. They might try to appeal to a new audience and alienate their existing customer base. They might lose focus and fall behind competition by failing to keep up with changes in their behaviour.

Successful brands of the future will focus on serving their audience consistently, as has always been the way. They will meet their needs and anticipate future changes in their wants and behaviours. By staying in regular contact and checking the pulse of their chosen market they will create a loyal tribe of people who live the brand.

There is no room for boring, same old brands in modern economies. There are two camps. Loved or hated. Those in the middle are falling away, holding on for dear life while slowly but surely dying. Those that are hated, well they still seem to get customers with cheap deals and poor customer service, but the less said on that the better. They're driven by price and will always have a business as long as they can continue to make a profit on the lowest price in the market.

Those that are loved however are being rewarded. They're the brands of the future. They consistently serve their audience. They innovate. They make the customer experience better and consistently deliver on their brand promise to their audience by adding value to their lives.

Is marketing unethical?

Currently? Yes.

Technology should have made marketing more ethical. With access to tools and tactics that make reaching our target audience easier than ever, the opportunity to use it for good is huge.

While lots of people are using technology for good, marketers have taken it upon themselves to use it to interrupt people more often.

Marketing is being used to take away our attention, to interrupt us as we try to focus on other more important things in our lives.

Social media is a prime example. What should be about connecting people has been turned into an advertising platform full of brand posts promoting products and services.

Unethical marketing

Despite the rise in the number of brands adopting ethical stances, unethical marketing is alive and kicking. Here are a few examples of tactics being employed by unethical marketers today.

- **Creating false scarcity to bolster sales with social proof apps**

  Social proof is an amazing thing, giving brands a chance to be transparent and use data to improve marketing KPIs, but high profile examples like Booking.com being investigated by the CMA are shining a light on some of the questionable uses of social proof in some companies' marketing.

- **Fake testimonials**

  A fair few B2B and B2C marketers are guilty of this one. Creating fake testimonials is one way to lose any credibility and trust that you have built with your audience.

- **Underdelivering and overpromising**

  Any marketer knows that underdelivering and overpromising leads to a frustrated customer. But even now, sales teams and marketing messages are over hyping products and services. Think Fyre Festival. You're not only disappointing customers, you're also being unethical.

Ethical marketing - is there such a thing?

The good news? Marketing doesn't need to be unethical. Ethical marketing is a thing and forward thinking marketers are using it to add real value to their customers.

The best marketers are adopting ethical marketing principles to win the trust and attention of their audience. This builds strong relationships with them, turning them into raving brand fans who become die hard customers.

CHAPTER 3
Trust and attention

Brand trust is one of the most important yet intangible assets that any business has, but every year brands are seeing themselves lose just a little bit more. This loss is often caused by a big scandal, a lack of care for customers or not following through on brand promises. However trust is lost, the results are still the same. A poor brand image, stunted business growth and ineffective marketing campaigns.

Consumers don't trust brands anymore

People don't buy from brands they don't trust. It's as simple as that.

A study by Ipsos Connect in 2017 found almost 70% of consumers don't trust advertising and 42% distrust brands.

Why don't we trust brands anymore? Brands have been behaving badly for years and getting away with it. So what's the difference now?

We all have access to a database of information updated in real time. Whether Sally down the road got ripped off when she bought her new washing machine or your colleague shared an article on Facebook about Dyson leaving the UK to move their headquarters to Singapore after campaigning for Brexit, it all has the same effect.

It's empowered us all to make our own decisions. Taking in the information we have available to us and making our own mind up.

Yes, advertising and marketing still work and they have a big influence on our buying decisions, but beliefs and ethics have become an even bigger part of our decision making process to guide who to buy from.

As soon as a brand does something that goes against its own marketing message, doesn't live up to its brand promises or behaves in a way that doesn't sit well with us - the damage is done and trust is broken.

With all this information it's pretty easy to pick up on BS. For years businesses have been faking purposes and backing causes that don't really fit with their brand. Connectivity and technology have exposed them as the PR campaigns they really are.

Building a relationship

Gaining trust isn't actually that difficult. It takes time, something that a lot of brands aren't willing to commit.

Trust can be built in brands the same way it is built in a personal relationship.

Know yourself and be real: the cliché "you can't love someone until you love yourself" applies to business too. Until a brand knows who it is and what it stands for it doesn't stand a chance of people loving it too. We've all been through relationships where we thought we were getting to know someone and it turns out it was all a show and they're actually a bit of a waste of space. Brands have been doing just that for years, overpromising and underdelivering.

Ensure your actions match your words: this is where most brands are falling down and losing trust, they say one thing and do another. We all know that's going to end in heartbreak.

Take time: you don't ask for marriage on a first date but a lot of brands do this in their marketing. Brands don't invest enough time in building a relationship with their audience. How can you trust someone when you know their intentions are purely to make some money from you?

Open communication: organisations are still holding onto the old days where you could push out marketing messages and people either bought or didn't buy. Everyone has a voice and each of us has a platform to share our opinions, whether they're good or bad. Brands need to be open in the way they communicate and be more willing to take feedback from their audience.

Is it too late to repair damage to brand trust?

Yes, for some brands it's too late. Just like in relationships, sometimes you can't rebuild that trust. Perhaps they should have behaved properly in the first place?

But there is still hope to build trust in other brands by starting to look at the way they do business.

Become value driven: rather than inventing brand stories, businesses should be looking at the values of their business. Brands that are driven by their values and use them to make decisions will thrive. Does this fit with our values? No. Don't do it. Instead of inventing brand stories find out what's important to customers and employees and use it to develop brand values that the brand can live by.

Follow through on promises: nothing breeds more distrust than saying something and doing the opposite. Trust is built by consistently delivering on promises.

Be more transparent: brands need to let people see inside the business, they shouldn't feed them press releases and filtered versions of what's going on. Consumers love getting to know the brands they buy from - sharing posts from employees or behind the scenes photos make a brand more human.

Without trust there is no business

The brands who will succeed in years to come despite shifts in demographics, markets and other outside influences will be those who build a healthy relationship with their audience. The key to a healthy relationship? Building trust and keeping it.

The most valuable commodity you have is your audience's time

You need to remember this when you're marketing. We must treat other people's time as if it were our own -   seconds, minutes and hours that person will never get back.

The most valuable commodities we can earn as a marketer are trust and attention. Once you've earned their attention with a winning message that resonated you need to earn their trust by delivering on the thing that caught their attention.

If you offer a free consultation, make it the best consultation they've ever had. If you offered a free ebook, make sure it's valuable.

Once you've won someone's attention, don't treat it like a marketing metric, treat it as if it were your own attention. Use it to add value to that person's day.

We're fickle

With so much information and choice, we've become a fickle bunch.

When we search for a product we're interested in, we're bombarded with five ads at the top of Google, followed around by retargeting ads on social media and your best mate Becky throws her opinion round like a discus thrower at the Olympics.

This makes the buying decision a hundred times harder and when we find decisions hard, we tend not to make the decision. We get distracted or overwhelmed and the chance to improve that person's life with your product or service is lost.

Your message and your marketing needs to align perfectly with your target's thinking at that time and earn their attention despite the hundreds of distractions that might stop them making the choice to buy from you.

Don't dissapoint

People don't buy from brands they don't trust. It's as simple as that.

If you've been to a traditional used car sales showroom, you'll know the tactic "overpromise and underdeliver." You're promised the world and the reality is disappointing. The same can be said for marketing. Advertising promises the latest features and guarantees, then when the product arrives it's disappointing and doesn't meet the expectations set by the advertisement.

Now I'm not saying you should underpromise and overdeliver. You still need to win someone's attention - but do it honestly. Don't overpromise. Do overdeliver.

As consumers we're fine tuned to detect BS nowadays because of the number of disappointing product and service purchases we've made. It will take time and more marketers choosing the right way to market to rebuild that consumer trust in marketing, but it can be done and if you choose to be ethical with your marketing and advertising your audience will reward you with their trust.

Earn attention quickly

Jamie wants to gain muscle, Kate wants to look stunning for her wedding, Adam wants to find Mr Right, Dwaine wants to look younger.

We have the same basic needs as we did hundreds of years ago. The difference now is the sheer number of people trying to fulfill those needs. Going back to the previous chapter, there are too many people doing the same thing in most industries. They're all using ads and they're all pedalling the same message to try and win a sale.

Be different

From an early age we're taught to fit in. Schools teach children to fit into categories, we're taught a very specific curriculum with very little wiggle room for creative and experimental thinking. We're taught to fit into social groups, we pick subjects based on what we're good at not what we enjoy and we're expected to go to university and take a traditional career.

We spend life after school trying to find ourselves. Experimenting with fashion, drugs, alcohol and sexuality to find out who we are after years of being suppressed by a system churning out robots.

If you're in marketing, you've done better than most. You're working in an amazing industry filled with creative people and ideas. It's your chance to be different.

The easiest way to earn attention? Being different to others in your space.

Now is your time to stand out and find your unique space in the world. You can create a business around what makes you unique. You can find a tribe of people who are different too. A tribe that is looking for the product or service you can bring to the world.

By being different to others in your industry you can stand out. Injecting personality into marketing is the easiest way to stand out and win the attention of the right people you need to attract.

CHAPTER 4
Make marketing more human

I've talked a lot about demographics and similarities in consumers but really we're all individual with a unique set of goals, dreams, values and beliefs. Whilst it would be impossible to create a company that catered for every person's unique set, we can find the smallest possible market for our brand with a close alignment of values to build strong foundations for a successful brand.

Short term marketing focus is ruining marketing

A 2016 report based on analysis of around 500 case studies entered into the IPA's Effectiveness Awards found 47% of brands communication budgets are now spent on short-term marketing activation strategies, up from 31% in 2014.

You could understand marketers moving their money to short term marketing activity if it was effective but according to the IPA marketing campaigns' ability to create brand fame and contribute to profit growth has been falling since 2009 with levels of effectiveness lower than the were a decade ago.

Short term marketing focus is just that. Short term focused. Often short sighted and focused on bringing in quick sales wins. The problem with this approach? It doesn't focus on building long term brand value, short term sales activation is often driven by discounting and advertising which are having a negative effect on the bottom line and brand loyalty.

In order to thrive, long-term brand building versus short-term sales activation needs to be rebalanced with a shift back to brand building campaigns that provide real value to audiences.

Acting like a human

"There's nothing I can do."
"I'm sorry but it's company policy."

We've all been on the phone to a customer service advisor who has said these words.

Monotone brands are going to fail and quickly. Barriers to entry in most markets are at their lowest and direct to consumer brands are disrupting established brands.

Let's take Casper, the American boxed mattress company. They grew to $750 million in sales in 4 years. Pretty impressive. They moved away from discounting and the traditional sales driven mattress selling process, instead opting to focus on quality and create an enjoyable brand experience.

It's hard to believe before the rise of the direct to consumer mattress providers, we had to visit furniture stores, find what type of mattress we wanted, choose a size and then be sold whichever was the most profitable for the showroom salesperson to sell you on the day. That's even before you had to wait weeks for the delivery driver to find your bedroom.

Casper reinvented the buying experience by giving the customer the power, removing unnecessary steps and creating a more enjoyable experience for what should be a nice purchase. Lindsay Kaplan, Casper's VP of communications and brand engagement said, "Our strategy from the start has been to change perceptions about mattress shopping and create a community around sleep in a playful and creative way, with a genuine voice."

Brand solutions solve real people's problems. That's the way brands should be run.

Brands have been so driven by profit, systems and processes they have forgotten as marketers and entrepreneurs they're dealing with people.

Decide what sort of brand you want to be. Do you want to be a lifeless zombie brand stumbling from customer to customer or do you want to be a brand people love, creating a meaningful relationship by serving your audience?

Business to human

Forget B2B and B2C. Think B2H.

Business to human is the new norm across most industries. The lines between B2B and B2C are blurring faster than ever with millennials now taking up managerial and director level roles in organisations. Decision makers within B2B brands are human, something a lot of salespeople tend to forget when they're pitching to other businesses.

In 2018 Forrester conducted research that found consumers who perceive your brand as human are 2.1 times more likely to love the brand and 1.9 times more likely to be satisfied by it. Consumers who perceive a brand as human are 1.6 times more likely to purchase from that brand and 1.8 times more likely to recommend it.

What characteristics make us human? How can we utilise them to make our brand more human.

Storytelling, complex emotions and creative thinking are just a few of the things that make us human. When your brand utilises just a couple of these unique human characteristics you are helping to humanise your brand and make it more appealing to your audience.

Who would your brand be if it were a person?

Marketing is the connection between a consumer and a brand, it enables a two way conversation   between audience and brand. Thinking of your brand as a person makes it much easier to visualise how that conversation might go.

- How would you talk to another person?

- What sort of language would you use?

- What colours would you wear?

- What core beliefs would drive your actions?

- Is your brand a Kim and Kanye or more of a Greta Thunberg or David Attenborough?

Define is all about defining who you are as a brand and finding people who care. By visualising your brand as a person you can find people who would want to engage and be friends with you. Your brand needs friends to survive. It needs people who love it, just like humans need other humans to survive and thrive.

Become immersed in your market

You can't expect your audience to live and breathe your brand if you don't live and breathe it for them.

Get to the heart of the market you want to change, because until you really understand how it works currently and how you want to change it you don't stand a chance of success. You need to understand the motivations of the current buyers in the market and identify ways you can improve the experience for them.

If you're looking to establish a new concept, you need to find real problems people are facing and get under the skin of what would motivate these people to choose you to solve their problem. The only way to do that is to dedicate your time to listening and understanding the market.

In 2009, Airbnb founders Joe Gebbia and Brian Chesky were stuck. Their concept wasn't catching on and they weren't getting enough homeowners to sign up as hosts or visitors to stay in homes. They decided to go on tour and stay with some of the hosts they had already signed up, and while they were staying in cities they held roadshow events to meet people face to face to see what concerns they had about the sharing economy and more specifically Airbnb's concept. They immersed themselves in their business and met early adopters to understand how they could address their needs. Since then the business has gone onto a valuation of $35 billion. If the founders had not taken the time and initiative to meet their audience and find out how to better serve them, they probably wouldn't be where they are today.

Personalised ads are still just advertising

When marketers talk about personalisation we talk about tailored social advertising or behavioural marketing. Whilst targeted ads might be good for marketing metrics, consumers are sick of seeing poorly designed adverts with no relevance to their core values and needs.

They're sick of seeing product driven advertising selling them the latest shiny thing they don't need in their lives.

Social advertising is pretty clever. Facebook and Instagram allow us to target people by age, location, gender, new job role, moves to a new area, anniversaries and financial status. Whilst that raises its own ethical questions (Think Cambridge Analytica Scandal), it's a pretty good tool to target people with advertising.

That said. Personalised targeting is essentially still just advertising. A 2018 report by YouGov found 55% of British adults say personalised adverts creep them out.

Marketing is about aligning yourself with a specific audience and existing to serve them in any which way you can, whilst making a profit. Targeted advertising obviously fits into that, but if you believe the hype of the Facebook Ads experts you'll believe that Facebook Ads is going to make you the next billionaire overnight.

It's more important than ever that organisations match their marketing to their consumers rather than specific campaigns and tactics like personalised marketing.

The likes of Seth Godin have pushed marketers for years to stop the scattergun approach to marketing and really personalise it. It seems organisations listened and have moved to producing more targeted advertising.

But, in The Reality Report 2019 study of over 287,000, 90% of consumers describe targeted ads as 'annoying'.

We're getting sick of seeing the same companies spending money on delivering message after message into our lives.

Beyond traditional segmentation

We're all unique. Just because you're a 20 something doesn't mean you're going to care about the environment and lefty politics. It's not fair to generalise in branding and marketing. We must be careful around how we use segmentation and move away from stereotypes to a more personal way of identifying our target audience.

Shared beliefs go beyond demographics and some of the segmentation methods used by brands is questionable at best. Think about the way you segment your audience. If you opened up your processes to your audience how would they feel about the way you profile them.

Big brands like Procter & Gamble (P&G) have moved away from generic audience demographic data based on gender and age groups to a more streamlined "smart audience" approach including first-time mums and first-time washing machine owners. This has allowed the fast-moving consumer goods (FMCG) giant to personalise their marketing to better address the needs of specific audiences.

In a 2019 Marketing Week survey of more than 800 marketers, behaviour, location and age were identified as the three biggest segmentation criteria used by marketers. 91% of the marketers questioned said that behaviour was the most effective method of segmentation in recent campaigns.

Personal interests and life stage are being used increasingly more in marketing segmentation and rightfully so. Segmenting audiences with similar interests and life stages allows you to personalise marketing at a deeper level, addressing the different needs of specific audiences.

There may be similarities between groups of people and their interests but it's important to remember that no two people are the same and everyone wants to feel unique. Make them feel that way by serving them and their specific needs.

Human centered brands start with personas

Segmenting based on based on the beliefs and values of your audience rather than age, gender or race is becoming more common. Which is great, but what do you do once you've segmented your audience into categories?

Produce buyer personas.

They've been around for a long while now in the marketing world but they're still not adopted by smaller marketing teams and tend to be reserved for larger organisations. Why? Perhaps because they seem like an easy step to skip when putting together marketing plans.

Buyer personas are perhaps one of the most helpful tools you can use as a marketer. Many companies who exceed revenue and lead goals have documented buyer personas.

A buyer persona is a visualisation of your target customer. It should be written as if this person is real and given a name. Some examples of persona names might include "First Time Mum Sara" or "Sustainable Adventurer Andrew." Personas should include as much detail about your target audience as possible, it should include demographic details about income, location and family alongside information about their motivations and problems.

Successful brands have multiple personas within their wider audience, so to save time when you've segmented a specific sub audience you should create your own buyer persona template.

Your buyer persona template should include headings like: name, overview, demographics, challenges or pain points, biggest fears, goals and motivations, hobbies and common objections.

Having personas in place for your audience will help guide messaging and future marketing campaigns. By getting super specific with who you're targeting you can better speak to your customers needs and wants, allowing you to cut through the noise and reach your audience more effectively.

Balancing automation with human interaction

Marketers have a multitude of tools at their disposal, from AI to chat bots. Marketing automation is common in most industries, according to 2019 research by Emailmonday 51% of companies currently using Marketing automation.

With the power to automate comes responsibility. Technology must not replace human interaction or even imitate it. Being open about automation is key to building an ethical brand. Those who put human connection and data privacy at the centre of their marketing strategy will stand the test of time and be on the right side of the technology vs humans argument in years to come.

How should marketing automation be used? Should we be using automation to free up more time to build better 1-2-1 relationships with our customers? What tasks should be automated? These are important questions you should be asking yourself and ones that shouldn't be taken lightly.

Instead of replacing humans, automation needs to be used in scenarios that work for the customer and the brand. According to the 2011 Lead Response Management Study, waiting more than 10 minutes to follow up decreased the odds of securing a lead by up to 400%. Automation can speed up the first touch.

Humans only have so much time in their day. Using email automation to let someone know you have their enquiry alongside some helpful information or content links could be the difference between winning a sale and losing it to a competitor.

Consumers want brands to use technology to provide a more personal service. This means you need to find the right balance between automation and personalisation. Technology has its place but choosing when and how to use it is a considered and important decision to make.

CHAPTER 5
Branding drives change

When you get branding right everything works. Changes in culture and behaviour, increases in charitable donations and reductions in carbon emissions.

When a brand gets it right, the possibilities for delivering their vision are endless. Without branding the chances of delivering that vision are pretty slim. Why? Because ideas don't catch on without branding.

Ideas don't catch on without branding

A combination of brand strategy and identity can bring about positive change in the world.

For years branding experts sold branding as a way to sell more product and increase brand choice and loyalty. While this is true and branding has a huge impact on the profitability and success of a brand, the real impact of branding is on the change it brings about on behalf of organisations. A brand multiplies the impact of an idea, it takes an idea and makes it digestible and shareable.

It helps us to decide which brands to align with, which brands we buy from and which charities we support. We have branding to thank for the reduction in stigma around HIV, the success of Comic Relief and for a general increase in donations to charities.

Without branding ideas would stay as ideas, they would never achieve their potential to reach millions of people across the world.

A story to buy into

Branding is a complicated business incorporating positioning, brand strategy, identity design and messaging. But at its most basic, branding is the process of communicating something. An idea. A cause. A purpose.

That idea is communicated through brand positioning and design to help people to understand the message and categorise it accordingly. Visual clues and typography contribute to the brain associating and remembering that message.

And the best way to be remembered? Tap into emotion, into the dreams and aspirations of your audience.

The best brands belong to their audience, they exist to serve their audience. They're customer and story driven. They make us feel something. Think Patagonia, the NHS and Macmillan. They create an authentic story around the brand. They then take that story and make it ours. It's not about the brand anymore it's about us. The brand belongs to us. We feel passionately about its success.

They lead the conversation in their industry. They move the industry forward and they drive change and real value by existing. That's the power of a story.

Don't misuse branding

Craft an authentic story based on the truth. Your audience isn't stupid, they have a wealth of tools available to them to investigate a brand. We can pick up on when a brand means what they say and when they don't.

Your brand is your promise to your audience. Don't misuse their trust and attention. Brand equity is lost every time you don't deliver or you don't live by the standards you've set out as a brand.

Research before action

For years marketers relied on assumptions to make business decisions, now there is a wealth of data available to marketers and business owners to help make important marketing decisions.

When most people think about branding they think about the visuals, the fonts and the logo of a brand. While these are all important, they are all the products of a great brand strategy. These assets become the face of the company but there's so much more beneath the surface making a brand work and deliver.

Without proper research you'll have a great product or service without anyone to buy it. Build it and they'll come just isn't true. The best brands are carefully crafted to immerse themselves within an audience or market segment to solve the problems that keep people up at night.

For existing brands, the easiest way to check your branding is consistent and working is to perform a branding audit. Look / Hear / Act.

Look: does your brand fit in your market? Does it say what you do? Does it use colours and imagery that communicate your message effectively?

Hear: your brand has a voice. How do you respond to feedback on review sites? How do you write company blogs? Is your tone of voice resonating with your target market?

Act: how does your brand behave currently? Does it have a set of values it uses to make decisions? Does it consider its impact on others and the environment?

Think Look, Hear, Act when you think of your brand. If any of these three areas are out of sync, it may be time to look at how you improve them to create a more impactful brand.

If you're performing poorly in all three areas it might be time to start thinking about a rebrand. Rebrands can help companies successfully reposition themselves to better serve their audiences. Macmillan is a great case study for rebranding, increasing revenue to over £120 million per year since their rebrand.

For startups and those of you without a brand, research should be the starting point of any branding campaign. Before you jump into strategy or design, research your market and audience. Craft your brand around your audience to create a brand for them, not for you.

Your research will drive your brand strategy and identity.

Building a brand

Research: The existence of too many businesses is partly down to a lack of research at the brand development stage of a brand launch. If brands did more research, they'd know the market was already saturated and there wasn't a desire from customers for another brand with similar or identical products and services.

Every branding project should start by investigating and researching the issues in your chosen market, identifying the levels of competition and deciding if your solution is right for the problems in that industry. Finding out where the brand should sit in a market is another key part of the research stage.

Strategy: This is the nitty gritty of a brand. Your core purpose is defined at this stage along with messaging to communicate the purpose. The strategy stage is key to the success of a brand, jumping straight to the design phase is a mistake made far too often.

The outcome of this phase should be a clear reason for your brand existing. One that gives you a real reason to serve your audience. Everything from your name to taglines and visions should be defined in your strategic planning. Preparation at this stage will help the design process run as smoothly as possible.

Design: This is the fun part and usually the bit that everyone thinks about when they think about branding. The design of a brand is an enjoyable process, one where the research and strategy phases play out and brings together a coherent brand identity. Done well, the design of a brand identity can make your brand famous amongst your audience and act as a marker of everything you stand for.

Implementation: Implementation of a brand is usually the downfall of new brand launches, the research has been well thought out and the design expertly executed but if the implementation is poor, the brand will fall flat.

This stage is another that's often forgotten by marketers. The successful adoption of a brand needs a plan, it needs to be communicated internally and externally for maximum impact. You should plan how your new brand will be rolled out in a way that everyone involved understands.

The key to a successful branding project is following a set process from start to finish. It can be tempting to skip past stages or rush certain elements, but taking your time and doing your research will result in a brand that stands the test of time, connects with your audience and delivers profitable growth.

Perceptual and positioning mapping

Perceptual and positioning maps form the basis of a market positioning strategy for products or services. They can be used by existing brands to map where their products and services are positioned in the market or by new brands to identity gaps in the market they can fill.

An example of a positioning map for car brands might include one axis labeled cheap and expensive, and another axis that might be labelled luxury and sports. Each car manufacturer will occupy a space on these axes. Porsche might occupy a space in the luxury expensive category.

When a new car manufacturer called Tesla came along, they created a new axis, electric cars. They took themselves out of the normal positioning thinking and created a new category.

As the industry becomes established they will need to relook at their positioning with new axes to determine their space in the market and which space in a customer's mind they want to occupy.

You need to occupy a clear space in your audience's mind. If your brand sits in the same space as your competitor brand you'll be seen as the same, leaving little differentiation besides price.

Do your research once you've identified a gap. There may be a reason why others don't occupy that space. A cheap luxury car for example might be a quick way for a manufacturer to go out of business.

Positioning is an essential part of branding and should be a key part of your brand creation process. Having a clear position in your audience's mind is essential.

Branding boils down to "why are we here?"

Your customers need you to add real value. They need to understand why you exist.

Don't overcomplicate it and don't be a me too cause (NB I don't mean the #MeToo movement when I refer to a me too cause. I'm referring to adding on causes used by other brands). Move beyond statements like "I want to save the planet," and be specific and simple with your why. Don't stunt your ambition but do be realistic about the impact one organisation can have in the world.

You should produce a mission statement and tagline but instead of filing it away as a never to be seen again document, live by it. Let your why guide every decision you make. If an action doesn't align with your why, don't do it.

In business and marketing, we're often asked to take on new projects and opportunities. It's easy to get lost in a sea of everything other than the thing we want to be doing. Use your why to dictate your yes and no answers. Does it get you closer to achieving the change you want to make? No? Turn it down.

You need to be able to communicate your why in less than a minute. I've lost track of the number of networking events I've been to where I'm either none the wiser as to what someone does or I'm completely turned off because it's a load of waffle.

Communicate your why consistently and passionately with an elevator pitch. If you're like me you might cringe at the phrase but having a consistent way to communicate your brand's reason for existing is important to connect with and serve your audience. People are time poor and the quicker you can get across your brand message, the quicker you can start serving those who care.

Be good at one thing

Why do brands with early success fail? Whilst there are lots of reasons, perhaps one often overlooked is that they keep adding to their offering which dilutes their own brand.

Be good at one thing and extend your offering when your audience asks you to. Don't presume your audience wants more just because you do. Traditional business thinking would have you believe that once you have a customer you should milk them for all they're worth, by adding services and products until they can't spend any more with you.

But by adding to your offering you can confuse your reason for existing. By adding misaligned products you're putting profit before purpose. Even worse, if you haven't perfected one thing, how can you be perfect at something else?

This is particularly true for technology companies. They get early traction and adoption with a simple MVP (minimum viable product), they continue adding more and more features which in time complicate the product offering. Customers will then leave to go to a new brand offering a simple approach. The cycle and customer churn continues.

Be good at one thing and build from there, if you think of a new product or service that might benefit your audience, wait until the time is right to launch it. Perfect the brand you have before you try to extend it.

Build your why into a manifesto

An easy way to ensure you live your brand? Create a manifesto.

Typically, a brand manifesto describes why your organisation exists. It should include your values, why you exist, who you're here to serve and what you will and won't do to reach your goal. Brands like Nike, Apple and Patagonia all have brand manifestos.

Your audience isn't just made up of potential customers, it's made up of your future employees. The best brands have principles they live and die by. On the wall of Gymshark HQ you'll find "GET SHIT DONE – DON'T BE A DICKHEAD –NOT TALENTED, OBSESSED" written on the wall. These statements are used to show existing and potential employees what they're about. Simple statements like this can keep a brand going when the going gets tough. They also help humanise a brand to build relationships with their future workforce and customers.

Brands are cliques with purpose

Successful brands don't appeal to everyone, you'll turn some people off when you're doing branding right. That isn't something to be scared of, it's something to be proud of.

If you've successfully researched, designed and built a brand you will spark conversation and debate. Not everyone will get it, not everyone will want to be a part of your journey. And that's okay. It means you've done your job right. You've created a brand that speaks to a specific group of people.

Branding is a vehicle for delivering the change you wish to make. There's only so much room in one car, you're going to have to leave some people behind if you want to make a difference in the world.

CHAPTER 6
Market to people who actually care & stick with it

The trouble with marketing is that most people don't care about what you want to say.

We've established we're all busy and lead increasingly stressful lives so how do we make life easier for ourselves as marketers and entrepreneurs?

Market to people who actually care about what you have to say. By doing research and strategic planning to find an audience that fits our message and purpose, it becomes much easier and less expensive to reach our audience. Our marketing cuts through the noise of all the other brands trying to get noticed and gets directly to the people who care about what we have to say.

Stop pestering people who don't care

People laud digital marketing as a saviour to marketing. Marketers constantly brand traditional marketing as being dead. Print is dead. TV advertising is dead. The list of marketing strategies and tactics that are dead is longer than a rambling Donald Trump tweet.

The truth is we're constantly sold new ways to market as a way to solve our marketing problems.

Marketers are obsessed by shiny things. AI, chatbots, Facebook Messenger, VR... the list of saviours of the marketing industry is endless. Yet successful marketers are still using print and other traditional marketing tactics to market their brand profitably.

How? Because marketing tactics aren't the problem.

If you have a marketing problem, I'm 99% sure it's not a problem with a tactic. It's more likely a problem with...

A) The people you're targeting.

B) Your marketing message.

Or both.

When you boil down any successful marketing campaign and brand it all starts with these two things. You're either pushing the right message to the wrong people, pushing the wrong message to the right people, or you're pushing the wrong message to the wrong people. You've got a real problem if you're doing that last one!

The problem with shiny marketing tactic syndrome is you're still pestering people who don't care about you or your brand. They don't care what your latest product does. They don't care if you've not heard from them in 6 months. They don't care if you're about to go out of business because you're losing money.

But they do care about something. It's your job as a marketer and entrepreneur to find people who do care about your brand. It's your job to serve them and create a brand that connects with them, solves their problems and helps them be a part of the change they want to see in the world.

Get focused, forget the masses

As a marketer for businesses small and large, I often ask the question "who is this product for?" "who is your customer?" The most common answer I get is "everyone."

Seriously.

People still say this.

But it's not their fault. It's a naivety based on the success stories of others. Overnight success stories make us believe that it's easy to make millions from our business idea by targeting the masses. But in reality, those success stories didn't happen overnight, those businesses spent years perfecting their product and service for early adopters, they've been through many hundreds of iterations and have pivoted to target different customers countless times.

They didn't start out trying to please the masses. It might be a byproduct of the work they've put in up to now but they definitely didn't start out by targeting everyone.

Everyone is not your customer.

Most startups fail within their first 5 years because they run out of money. What's the quickest way to run out of money? Spending more money than you're getting in. And usually the quickest way to spend money? Marketing.

If you're in business you're likely in competition with brands with a bigger marketing budget than you. They have deep pockets. They have millions to throw at marketing their brand. So why are you trying to compete? You're trying to go after the same people as they are with a fraction of their resources.

It's time to get focused and forget the masses.

By focusing your marketing spend on reaching a specific group of people who care about your brand, you're setting yourself up for success.

Get out of the middle of the road

Targeting everyone means you can't upset or offend anyone. You can't be unique. You have to blend in. You have to be middle of the road and in the age of information overload and generic marketing messages we really don't need any more boring brands thrown into the mix.

Middle of the road leads to me too brands.

"I offer a quality service." "My product is better quality." "I provide a better service." We see these brand promises everyday. What do we do? We ignore them because every other business in that space says the same thing.

The middle of the road is exciting for lots of businesses because it's where everyone else is. It's where they think the action is.

But let's think of the road as a 70mph dual carriageway. We wouldn't go and stand in the middle of that road. Cars passing us on both sides at 70 miles per hour. We'd want to get to the side of the road as quickly as we could. This is the same as marketing. All those cars are your competitors, all going in one of two directions, following each other, competing with each other for space on the road.

By standing at the side of the road, you're standing at the edges.

The edges are where you need to be as a brand. The edges of your market. Pushing to create some breathing room for you and your brand.

That's what focus does.

Focusing on a smaller market of people who care gets you from the middle of the road to a place of safety. Away from bland. Away from boring and away from your competition.

Blue Ocean Strategy

If you haven't read the book Blue Ocean Strategy by Renée Mauborgne and W. Chan Kim. Go get it.

The book talks about red and blue oceans. Red being the oceans most businesses are swimming in, the markets that already exist. Those with lots of competition. Competitors try to outperform their rivals to get a bigger slice of the existing customer demand in the industry. Growth and profits are reduced as a result. The competition is fierce, almost like a blood sport with lots of blood spilt hence the red ocean analogy.

Blue oceans are new markets. Markets which aren't in existence yet. You create the demand instead of trying to compete with everyone else for the existing demand. The potential for growth and profits in blue oceans is huge.

This is a really simple overview of the book and it obviously goes into a lot more detail about the strategy and ways you can use it in your business. Case studies of brands like Cirque du Soleil who used Blue Ocean Strategy to create their own demand are testament that the strategy works.

In pretty much every industry there are too many businesses competing for too few customers. If you you want to be swimming in the blue ocean with less competition rather than competing with lots of others you need to be using Blue Ocean Strategy and the Serve Marketing Manifesto at the back of this book to push the boundaries and move to the side of the road to create your own space in your market. Be different and generate new demand for your organisation.

Be specific and be brave

Sometimes when I speak to businesses about marketing to a smaller group of people, they instantly think they're going to make less money, reduce their profit margins and be out of business in six months.

It's a normal response when someone says something that's the very opposite to what you've tried to do for so long. In a world that values revenue growth we're tuned to try and look big for opportunities and to focus on big numbers to deliver our ambitious growth targets.

But what if you could make more money and a bigger impact on people's lives working with a smaller group of people by serving a market of people who care?

You can.

Being specific is brave. Your colleagues might think you've gone mad. Your partner might think you're not thinking about the money. Your friends might say you're thinking too small.

But stick with it. Be specific with who you serve and those people will reward you in ways you haven't even thought about yet.

Serve your audience and help them deliver the change they want to see. They'll thank you. When you take the bold move to serve and lead people, you're repaid with invaluable feedback, sustainable growth, increased profits and a sense of belonging.

The smallest possible market

Trying to please everyone is the easiest way to create a bland, boring business that nobody cares about. The alternative is much better, creating a business that people love, one that they rave about to other people with shared interests and values. They will practically beg you to take their money because you're so valuable to them. They couldn't imagine you not being in business.

The days of everyone being your customer have all but ended, if they ever existed in the first place.

Yes your idea might grow to appeal to the masses but start by building a brand around people who care about something very, very specific.

Brands who have achieved global domination in recent years didn't start out with millions of customers. They started by finding smaller groups of people who were obsessed with a very specific problem.

Uber: found people who were sick of waiting for taxis, not knowing when they were turning up.

Deliveroo: found people who wanted restaurant quality food without having to stop watching Netflix.

Slack: found people who were annoyed by email communication and wanted a faster way to communicate with their team.

By focusing on a small group of people with a very specific problem they were able to build a community of fans who spread their story. Find people who are ready to listen to what you have to say. Tell them why you're the person to lead them to the solution and then do what you say you're going to do.

Find the fans you're willing to put the time in for

Business is tough, the stories of overnight brand success are a lie. Of course, every business is different and sometimes it's possible to make profits straight away with the right business model but on average a business will take 18 months just to break even. Multimillion dollar company MailChimp was founded in 2001, many many years of development and finding their way has helped them reach revenues of $700million, nearly 20 years after launching.

What's my point? No business is easy. No business is guaranteed success. If it was, everyone would be doing it.

You need to be willing to put the time in to make it a success. Working endlessly in your pursuit to make your business work. You're going to feel like you want to quit. Most people do.

That's why before you even start thinking about the fans, you need to look to yourself for guidance.

- What do you care about?

- What gets your blood flowing?

- What gets you angry/excited?

- What do you feel so passionately about that you'll stick with it?

You need to find a cause you feel passionate about. A pain point you feel so strongly about that you're willing to put the work in even when everything seems impossible. When nobody seems to be listening. When you're struggling and can't see how you're ever going to make this work.

Find the fans you're willing to put the time in for.

It's okay to say no

If you're already in business you've probably come across a customer you really shouldn't have signed up. That one awkward guy who takes up 80% of your day trying to fix issues that shouldn't be issues. The customer is always right. But sometimes the customer isn't right for you and your brand.

It's okay to say no to some people, that's the whole point of marketing to people who care. You can say thank you for your interest but I think you might be better working with Bob down the road.

By defining who you want to serve and who you want to help make a positive change, you save the hassle of signing up clients or customers you really shouldn't be working with.

If someone's values align with yours and your product or service is right for them, the relationship that grows can be astonishing. I class some of my marketing clients as friends now. I can call them if I need advice, they can drop me a text if they're having problems. When you're aligned with the audience you serve the results are amazing and the process is enjoyable, even when the work is tough.

Stand out or lose out

In chapter one, I talked about the fact that too many businesses exist.

It's true. If most businesses closed tomorrow the chances are you wouldn't even notice. In each industry there are the top players who win the majority of customers, projects or work. They pick up the customers they want and leave the rest of the market to scrap for the work they don't want.

Top branding agencies pick up the best clients and leave the awkward customer who wants to pay £10 for a logo design. The top accountancy firms win the biggest contracts and leave the small one woman band accountant to constantly chase late payments from the customer they don't like working with.

Create your own market. Be so unique you don't have any competition. Don't try to compete with the big boys in your market, you're going to lose. They have a lot more money and resources. Be as weird as you want to be and be as niche as you can with who you want to work with and what services you want to offer them.

In order to thrive, you need to stand out and stick to it. Don't be tempted to start watering your offering down to appeal to more people. If you do, you're heading back into the red oceans. You're competing on the same offering as others.

Be different. We're taught from an early age to conform. You can't do that. You can do this.

We're told not to touch certain things. We're told not to run. We're pushed by parents and teachers to pursue subjects that will give us a "safe" job. We're told to go to university.

But to succeed in business, you need to reverse years of that conditioning to fit in and to be like others. To succeed in today's business world we need to stand out. Not fit in.

Embrace your inner weirdo or unique values and build a business that reflects you. The world really doesn't need another boring me too business.

Don't use stick on values

You're working hard to find an audience that cares and you're ready to market to them. Don't be thrown off course by stick on causes. You know the sort. The brands saying they care for the environment despite pumping oil into oceans and paying workers pennies. Yes those. They're working hard to convince their audiences they're not just about making a profit. They create "authentic stories" to show us how they're on a mission to "make a difference."

The increase in the number of brands that have suddenly grown a conscience is creating a lot of noise around purpose and making it harder for brands who do care to cut through and connect with their audience to deliver their purpose.

Sustainability is a hot topic but it's important that brands recognise sustainability as a given, rather than a competitive advantage. In five to ten years' time, sustainability will be a necessary act of business, and if you don't do it, you vanish. You need unique values beyond things like sustainability and ethics.

Create a unique purpose for your brand. What do you care about? What does your audience care about? Don't be swayed by what everyone else is doing in business, your audience can see straight through a stick on cause. They want to know you're really serious about the issues they care about.

That's why choosing your values carefully as a marketer is essential. You need to care about the issues you're trying to solve else there's no point including them in your brand and marketing strategy.

Put a purpose at the heart of your brand and pick an original cause that is relevant to you, your brand and your audience. Deliver on that purpose. If you say you're going to reduce plastic waste, show people how you're doing it and report on the impact. If you say you're going to pay staff fairly, join the Living Wage programme. If you're going to give back a percentage of your time as a brand to good causes, show people on social media when you do it.

Use your unique purpose to drive your brand forward.

We don't need any more fluffy purpose statements. The world needs real action, unique values and purposes. Serve your audience and deliver the impact they want you to deliver.

Section 2: Communicate
Communicate your message effectively by living your purpose ethically
strategy, messaging, design, tools

Resource: The Communications Plan

On the following page you'll find a template for your communications planning. Use each column to plan each communication you make as an organisation. Identify who you want to talk to, what you want to say, how you should say it and when the message should be communicated. Planning communications allows you to deliver consistent on brand messages every time.

Who are we talking to?	What do we want to say to them?	How shall we say it?	When should it be communicated?

CHAPTER 7
Strategy and planning before tactics.
Always.

If you've searched the terms marketing, SEO or social media on Google recently you'll find a flurry of articles online with the best tactics to reach your audience with marketing tools.

While these articles are useful they're a little premature for most businesses. Most organisations are me too organisations, they do what their competitors do and flaunt claims like "quality service," "cheaper price," "better product." In reality consumers just see them as being the same as their competition with little to distinguish between them.

This is when people usually turn to reviews and recommendations because they find it hard to choose which company to choose to solve their problem. But what if your organisation could stand out from the get go? Be the preferred choice before a potential customer even starts to look at other brand choices?

To succeed, we need to start thinking about branding and marketing strategy before tactics. Stop thinking about social media, SEO and paid ads. Start thinking who am I serving and how do I need to speak to them to get my message across effectively?

What happens when you put tactics before a clear strategy?

Without a consistent brand message you're going to get lost in a sea of other brands in your sector. Without a clear idea of who you are, your customers are likely to be confused about what you offer and choose a competitor with a clearer offering.

Brands without a clear communications strategy often struggle to achieve their goals. You may know where you want to go but without a clear plan you'll be swimming blindly into a sea of better prepared competition. By using research, creativity and strategic thinking you can build a strategy that works for you and your audience.

You also waste your valuable marketing budget when you don't have a clear strategy in place. Taking the time to build a strategy by doing your research saves you a lot of wasted resource and money on the wrong messages and tactics to target your audience. A great marketer uses research to plan and spend their budget in the most effective way possible.

Finally, without a clear strategy the term "running around like a headless chicken" comes to mind. Without a strategy, your marketing efforts are unfocused and all over the place. Spend time to get focused on ways you can use your resources more effectively and you'll have a much more effective plan in place when you're ready to reach your customers.

Vision drives strategy

How will you achieve your vision?

You've set out your vision, the impact you want to have on the world and the change you want to deliver by existing. Great. Now you need a strategy. Your strategy is your guiding path to achieving your why. It sets out the steps you need to take to realise your ambition and purpose.

Allowing you to communicate your vision to everyone from your customers to shareholders and employees. It allows you to bring others along on your journey, to recruit your audience on that journey to achieving the impact you want to deliver.

Define, Communicate and Amplify

Marketing is treated like a promotional tool by pretty much everyone in business and it's the industry's fault. Marketers rolled over and let others shape the industry into an advertising focused mish mash of tactics. Marketing should be a joined up process incorporating all the separate break off industries.

Branding, design, strategy, communications, implementation and marketing need to be brought together in one brand to work. Marketing should bring together three key elements. Define, Communicate, Amplify.

The role of Define is to define the brand. Hopefully as you've progressed through the Define section of this book you've started asking some of the following questions:

- What are your core principles and values?

- What is your mission statement?

- Why do you exist?

- Who is your audience

- What do you want to come to mind when someone hears your business name?

- How do you behave as a brand?

Answering some of these questions as part of your drive to define your brand will make the Communicate and Amplify sections easy to understand and implement.

The role of Communicate is to identity what you want to say and how you're going to say it. You're going to need to really understand what sort of messages are going to cut through the noise and connect with your audience. You need to identify what tools you need to make those connections and more importantly you need a plan on how you're going to bring all these things together into a clear strategy.

I'll cover Amplify in more detail in the next section but it is about amplifying an impactful message to reach more people who care about what you have to say.

But first, let's put a plan in place to communicate with our chosen audience.

The elements of a communications plan

If you speak to different people you'll get a different answer to the "what do you include in a communications plan?" But I like to keep things simple and follow a who, what, how and when planning framework. All of your communications should be planned using this framework.

- Who are we talking to?

If you've read all of this book so far, you'll be a whiz at this section of your plan. Get specific about who you're talking to. In business you will have multiple stakeholders and people you need to communicate with, including shareholders, prospects, partners and suppliers. When you're writing your communications plan you should define exactly who you want to speak to.

- What do we want to say to them?

This is your key message. In the simplest terms what do you want to communicate? This shouldn't include fluffy marketing lingo, it should be a simple message you want to communicate to your audience.

- How shall we say it?

Will the communication be visual? Written? Video based? Choosing the method of communication is just as important as the message itself. Think about your intended audience. What would be the best way for them to receive your message? How can you do it in a way that doesn't interrupt them?

Tone of voice is also important here. Stick with your values, tone and personality when you're producing communications. How you say something is often more important than what you're saying.

- When should it be communicated?

Timing is everything in marketing. You need to think carefully about your audience's lifestyles and work lives for this stage. From the best time to post on specific social media platforms to the best days for email open rates, you need to make sure you're delivering your message for optimal impact.

There's not much point delivering a social media post at 3am if your audience is asleep. The social platform algorithms will pick up on the low engagement and your post will be hidden for nobody to see when they do wake up.

Planning communications is an important aspect that shouldn't be overlooked when you're planning marketing campaigns. By defining who, what, how and when - you will create more tailored, impactful messages to your audience.

Fail small

Be more startup.

Startups are great because they are agile and able to change course quickly without too much baggage. Pivoting is a well known phrase in startup culture, describing a change in business model or direction for the business. It can be applied to marketing. If a strategy isn't working, pivot. If the audience you've identified isn't responsive to your marketing message, maybe it's time to do more research to confirm your assumptions or perhaps you need to tweak your message.

By experimenting with marketing strategies you can test assumptions and treat your marketing as a science. Tweaking for the best results. The key is to fail small, don't spend thousands on projects, create an MVP (minimum viable product).

Sticking with your strategy

Don't lose focus of why you got into business, who you serve and the steps you need to take to get there.

You will get distracted along the way. Things will happen in your life, competitors will come into your space and you'll likely have a bout of Imposter Syndrome.

The worst thing a business or startup can do is flip flop between strategies. The result? A confused organisation stuck spinning its wheels with no clear direction or leadership. If you've done your research and identified a clear opportunity with a detailed understanding of who you're going to serve, you're on course to having a successful brand.

Now I'm not saying you should carry on blindly when a strategy isn't working. You need to constantly monitor your performance across marketing and the rest of the business but don't throw the towel in. Look at what tactics or messaging you could tweak to improve the progress you're making towards your goals.

Innovate but not for the sake of it

You need to be one step ahead of your competition. Successful businesses aren't looking at their next quarter, they're looking years ahead. What will be the next big innovation in their sector? How can they bring it to market before everyone else.

Define what innovation is to you. Why are you doing it? You might look to improve processes so you can offer a better customer experience or reduce your costs. You might innovate in customer service to better serve your clients.

Whatever it is, make sure you're innovating for the right reasons. Innovation for the sake of innovation is an easy way to waste time and money. Build time into your day for creative thinking. Empower individuals to bring new ideas to the table, whatever their department or seniority. Often those closest to the customer will have the best ideas based on sticking points or specific frustrations they have with your processes or systems.

Nominate someone in your organisation to be an innovation champion. The go to person for new ideas and innovation concepts. They can filter out the ones that don't add value and shortlist ideas worth pursuing to better serve your audience.

Your website doesn't need tweaking

There's no point making small changes if the bigger picture is broken. If you haven't got a clear message and proposition for your smallest viable market then your website is going to struggle. You're going to have to pay thousands of pounds to drive people to your site with advertising, most of that money will be wasted on people who don't care about your brand and the few people who do care will be put off by your generic, middle of the road message.

Unfocused brands constantly tweak their website content to make it look better, they use conversion optimisation software and pay Adwords/Facebook Ads specialists to drive lots of traffic to their site. Nothing works. No sales, no enquiries. Nothing. Shocker.

This might sound harsh but it's a reality for lots of small business owners and startups. They're me too businesses. They try to appeal to everyone and appeal to no one.

If you don't have a clear strategy to communicate with your audience it doesn't matter how much you spend on your website, it will fail.

If it ain't broke, don't fix it

In a wider business sense "if it ain't broke, don't fix it" is a stupid way to run your organisation. It's a sure fire way to be closing the doors if you're waiting around for your business to break. You need to anticipate when things are likely to break. Don't wait for it to break before you decide to fix it, you'll be playing catchup with your competition if you do. You need to keep up to date with new ways to serve your audience and provide better communication channels.

But when it comes to messaging, "if it ain't broke, don't fix it" works. If a message resonates and connects with your audience, don't mess with it. Don't try to tweak it to get an extra 0.14% increase in your conversion rate.

Marketers can get greedy or distracted and decide they want to add in new elements to their messaging, often confusing the ideas and sentiment behind the communication. If a message is helping you reach your objectives as part of your strategy, don't try to tweak it and change it. Stick with it.

Use data to shape messaging

Messaging is important at every stage in marketing from vision and brand to advertising copy and landing page calls to action. It's vital for the success of your brand and marketing campaigns.

Your messaging should be driven partly by creativity, partly by data.

You have a wealth of information available to guide your strategy. If you're looking to find the burning questions your audience needs answering, scroll down to the bottom of a Google search on a topic and you'll find related searches. This is free data giving you insight into what your audience is searching.

You can also use organic search data from software tools such as SEMRush or Moz Keyword Explorer to shape messaging. These give you data on searches and the questions your audience is asking. Look behind the data to the reasons why people are searching for specific terms and you'll have valuable information to use in your messaging.

Once you've sent out communications, whether it's a blog or social media post, you should be monitoring the response from your audience. Zero reaction or engagement is bad. Your message has flopped and hasn't connected. Find out why.

What was it about this specific post that didn't connect? Use free social media data and insights to look for trends in messaging that does and doesn't hit the mark with your audience. What posts are getting good engagement. What themes are there in these posts? Is the message similar? What do the comments say?

Another easy way to use data to shape messaging? Use Google Analytics. Which pages have a high bounce rate? How long are people staying on each page? What pages tend to see the longest visit duration? By looking into visitor behaviour you can get a clear understanding of what your audience is consuming and connecting with. Do more of what works and less of what doesn't with future communications.

Delivering a consistent message at every touchpoint

Perception of a brand is built through multiple interactions. Every interaction your customer has with your brand is a form of communication. Those interactions build into one big picture of how your customers see you. This picture guides whether or not they choose to buy from you now or again in the future.

Every stage should be considered from the customer's perspective. Will they need to fill their bin with excess packaging? Will they need to pay for their own postage if they need to return an item? Can they speak to someone from your organisation on the platforms they already use?

The strategy you've set for your brand, the way you speak to your customers and the messaging you want to get across to them should flow through every touchpoint. From the very first time someone becomes aware of your brand right through to a repeat purchase, you need to deliver a consistent brand experience that delivers on the promises you make to your audience.

CHAPTER 8
Giving back with your marketing

Brands should exist to serve their audience.

Successful brands of the future will turn up consistently, serving their audience for a sustained period of time. They'll be rewarded for their length of service with brand loyalty and a strong core base of die hard fans.

Your brand's very reason for existence should be to serve your audience.

Giving extends your life expectancy

Whilst giving back shouldn't be for selfish reasons, there is extensive research to show that giving back in business is good for you and your mental health.

If you've ever had a salivating meal, amazing sex or an engaging conversation - you've probably felt the rush of happy chemicals in your brain afterwards. The release of dopamine and endorphins makes us feel euphoric.

What if I told you generosity does the exact same thing to your brain? Whether you're giving time, money or being supportive of someone in need, your brain releases happy chemicals.

Moving beyond feeling good in the moment, the stress reduction associated with giving has been proven to reduce mortality risk linked to stress.

The reduction in stress and anxiety associated with generosity helps to reduce your lower pressure, lowering your risk of cardiovascular problems. All of these mental and physical benefits contribute to the direct correlation between philanthropy and increased life expectancy identified in a 2013 study published in the American Journal of Public Health.

The best thing? Unlike some other things that might make you feel euphoric, there's no come down and you don't have to pay for it. Being generous doesn't have to mean giving millions of pounds to charity either, as a marketer you're in a unique position to be able to give back in many ways.

You have the power to choose which charities your brand should align with, to make people smile by using your product and to make a positive change.

Imagine the feeling you'd get everyday knowing you're having that impact. Imagine the pride and enjoyment you'll get from knowing you're doing good in the world.

Use your power wisely

Marketers have the power to influence how people feel.

Don't abuse it.

For too long, marketers have used their power to influence others to twist, distort and create problems to sell products. Often marketers try to manipulate the way you feel to sell something. You didn't know you had a problem in the first place, so why did it become one that needed to be solved with a product or service? Marketing.

Now I'm not saying marketing shouldn't exist, else I wouldn't have written this book. But it needs to change. It needs to be used for good, for positive change.

Everyone has the power to affect people's days. The person who pushes to the front of the queue is affecting others who will have to wait longer. The person who uses their mobile phone whilst driving is risking the lives of others. The rude person who insists on speaking to the manager ruins the agents day.

The power you have as a marketer is amplified because of the reach of your actions. Social media amplifies your message and work. Content stays online for others to read. Your actions can influence the beliefs of others. Your actions can impact the health of children. They can influence the money someone has left over to pay their bills.

The list of the powers you have as a marketer are endless. The products you promote have an affect on people and the planet too.

If you're a marketer within a business, ask yourself if you're having a positive impact on people's lives by marketing the business you're working in. If you're a business owner, is your product having a positive impact on the health of people and the environment? If it's not, can you tweak it and use the power you have to do more good?

Giving back is good for business

Giving back to your audience can come in many forms, whether it's with charity partnerships or producing valuable content regularly.

It encourages word of mouth marketing: people like to tell people they're nice, whether we like to admit it or not. One of the reasons why people do good is to feel good about themselves and to be able to tell others. By creating an ethical product or service you're building that shareability into your business.

It attracts customers: By having shared values and beliefs running through your business and marketing, you're more likely to attract customers who share them and will buy your products and services because of it.

Brand loyalty: Have you ever noticed that brands who lead on ethics have developed a strong community with a tribe like mentality? That's because their customers have bought into the brand and its values. It's much harder to convince a customer to switch brands if they've got a more meaningful connection with their existing company.

Sometimes you can't measure the ROI

If you're a marketer you'll know the struggle. What's the ROI of this activity? What has this campaign done for the bottom line? Has it generated sales? Has it been a profitable strategy?

To get a seat at the top table in business marketing has had to evolve and develop to become a strategic and ROI driven activity. In a move away from the "branded pens and pads" department, we've finally got a seat in the boardroom. In lots of boardrooms across the globe marketing is finally getting the recognition it deserves as an important investable area of any business, whatever the industry.

But our success as marketers is having an unwanted side effect. Marketing activity that doesn't deliver an immediate ROI or result is being pushed aside for spending that delivers an immediate return. There's a tendency to focus on ROI from specific activity.

In reality, some things don't make money or deliver an ROI on spend but they contribute to the brand and future of it.

Joe Wicks aka The Body Coach is the perfect example of having a portfolio of activity and tactics that create value. Starting out by creating valuable content on Instagram he now has an app, cookbooks, regular TV slots and a YouTube channel. He might not get paid to go on This Morning but he knows that if he does he will sell more books and build authority with his audience.

Some people might say his videos on Instagram don't deliver an ROI but when you combine the Instagram videos into the overall strategy they contribute to the growth of his brand.

Most small business owners and marketers look at an activity and think "well that's a waste of time, I don't have time to spend three hours a week posting on social media." Now that might be true, but what if as part of a wider marketing strategy those three hours could drive new business and sales for years to come?

What if investing three hours a week, that's just six and a half days a year, could build awareness, connection and trust with your audience? Would it be worth investing your time then?

Sometimes activity doesn't make sense on its own. But combine it with an ecosystem of other activities, products and services and you have an unstoppable machine that works together to drive your message and business forward faster than any one part of your strategy on its own.

The power of free in your ecosystem

As a child I remember putting the Encarta 2000 CD-ROM into the huge computer tower and clicking through the information to do my homework, I couldn't have imagined then that at the time of writing there would be 1.2 trillion Google searches per year worldwide.

When Yahoo and Google came along and started offering that information free to people Microsoft probably thought they were stupid.

How can they give away such valuable information free? How are they going to make money? Why would they just give something away when you can charge for it like we do?

Google were thinking longer term. If they hadn't provided a free platform for those people who want up to date information, they wouldn't be generating $29.5 billion in revenue in 2019. They provided real value, free to the end user to generate huge revenues.

When the Coop opened where I live recently, they were handing out free cakes and vouchers. When the Costa Coffee opened around the corner, they sent two free coffee vouchers in the post. Not for the sake of it.

Why? Because free builds habits.

Free helps to build those unconscious habits. Think food. Think Coop. Think trainers, think Nike. Think dates, think Tinder. Think coffee, think Starbucks. All of these brands have used the power of marketing and free to become an unconscious decision in the minds of consumers.

We might think we're in control, but according to Dr. Emmanuel Donchin, director of the Laboratory for Cognitive Psychophysiology at the University of Illinois 95 percent of our brain activity is beyond our conscious awareness. We're literally walking through life unconscious. Dr. Robert Zajon, a social psychologist at the University of Michigan, noticed *"when people explain why they've made a decision, they are simply rationalising, attributing what sound like reasonable bases for what is in fact a murky, unknowable process."*

Free builds powerful subconscious habits.

Despite the huge success stories of people offering a valuable free product as part of a product ecosystem, business owners are still scared of "free". Any business can utilise the power of free. Whether it's giving away a free product to prospects, sharing ideas online or sending vouchers to potential customers.

Another super easy way to utilise free in your business? Give away your ideas. Charge for implementation. But if we give our ideas away, why wouldn't somebody just do it themselves? Most people don't have the time or the energy to do everything themselves.

Value comes with taking a pain away more quickly or better than they could themselves. To use the analogy of weight loss, the difference in cost between a set of dumbells and liposuction is huge. One you could do yourself with time, the other you have an instant result. People are willing to pay more for something that solves their problems more quickly or easier than doing it themselves.

Most people could probably tile their own bathroom if they watched a few YouTube videos. But do the majority of people do that? No. They hire a tiler because it's quicker and easier.

If you run a personal training brand, you might fit somewhere in the middle between a set of dumbells and liposuction in terms of cost and value, giving away a free session or arm workout online could be a good way to build trust and sell a higher ticket item further down the line.

If you're offering big ticket items or big risk items... free works great. You're providing value up front before someone is ready to work with you. Much better than traditional marketing, overselling and underdelivering, where you're expecting the buyer to take on all the risk to find if the product or service is right for them.

Free information, products and services give back and in turn build a stronger brand.

We make emotional decisions

Whether we like to admit it or not we make emotional decisions and back them up with logic. Despite millions of years of development our brains haven't really changed much.

Dr. Robert Zajon the social psychologist at the University of Michigan I mentioned earlier talked about the evidence showing we make emotional decisions and try to back them up with logic. So why are most marketers still focusing on product features and service levels? If buyers are making decisions based on emotion, why are we pushing how many widgets our machine has or how many colours our make up range has? Use emotion in your messaging.

In a 2014 study, the University of Glasgow found that our emotions stem from 4 core feelings; happy, sad, afraid/surprised, and angry/disgusted. We know marketers have and continue to use angry, afraid and sad as emotional levers to make buyers to take action. But what if we could use emotion more ethically?

Now I'm not saying you need to share photos of fluffy bears and memes 24/7. There needs to be a balance, like with the best films that take you on a journey with layers of emotion. From sadness to empathy and understanding to happiness and joy. Take your audience on a journey to somewhere more positive with your marketing.

Use emotions at different stages of the buying journey.

An easy way to engage the emotional decision making process is to share customer stories. They have been proven to activate the region of the brain that processes senses. If you're an ecommerce marketer, you could use user generated content. If you're a B2B brand, it could be a video interview with your customer sharing how your business has solved their problems.

Our brains are tuned to pick out the bits of information that resonate with our needs. Hearing, reading and seeing others share their experience makes us feel as if we're living the story, as if it happened to us already. That's pretty powerful and often makes the buying decision a lot easier to make.

Small kindnesses make a big difference

In a world of uncertainty and information overload it's time for us to remember what makes us human. As we approach a decade of autonomous vehicles and mainstream robotics, the very things that make us human will be the things that help us thrive.

Listening, understanding, empathy, awareness, kindness and emotion make us human. AI and robots can't replicate the things that make you who you are.

When you're no longer here, you won't be remembered because you improved conversion rate on your website by 1%. Your obituary won't mention how you grew your market share by 15%. It sounds harsh but nobody cares. People remember who you were as a person and how you behaved towards them and others.

If you're a marketer, startup or business owner you're uniquely placed to be kind. You have the chance to have a positive impact on someones day. Make the most of it by using small acts of kindness to give back with your marketing. Small kindnesses are remembered and are more important than ever in your personal and business life.

In marketing, the term moment of truth is used to describe the *"moment when a customer/user interacts with a brand, product or service to form or change an impression about that particular brand, product or service."*

These moments can come at any stage of a buyer's journey. From just becoming aware of your organisation to delivery and the post purchase review stage. Each moment is the perfect opportunity for you to give back with your marketing.

When you send out a delivery, add some free samples of other products you think the customer might like. When you email a potential prospect, do some indepth research and offer them some free advice to help them in their business.

When you mess up an order, refund the customer or arrange a redelivery without quibble. The customer doesn't care why you messed it up, they just want what they've ordered.

When the customer has just purchased, follow up with a series of tip emails to help them get the most out of your product. Don't just move onto the next sale and forget about them.

Focus on the moments of truth and opportunities to be kind.

Be more David Attenborough

> "No living person has done more to make the people of Planet Earth aware of the world around them" - Time Magazine, naming Sir David Attenborough 'Hero of the Environment' in 2007.

Everybody loves David Attenborough. Old, young, male, female, it doesn't matter who you are - you can't help but love him. Why? His charisma, expansive knowledge and dedication to help others understand the world we live in is infectious.

His influence on raising awareness of some of the most important issues of our time is astonishing. His impact on the climate change discussion, war on plastic and the destruction of habitats has forced industries to change, governments to introduce new policy and consumers to change their habits.

He didn't start out wanting to to save the world, it was a byproduct of his passion for TV and film. His constant drive to innovate and learn, showed him some of the things he now feels so passionately about. From seeing the destruction of forests to plastics in our oceans.

Whilst he was honing his broadcasting skills he came across some of the burning issues that affect us all and he saw it as his responsibility to take action and inspire others to do the same. He didn't just sit by and ignore important issues because it wasn't his job, he knew it was his duty to do something about it.

It's your responsibility to do the same. Have you noticed an issue that needs solving? Are you sick of seeing misleading marketing? Are you sick of seeing big corporations selling substandard products?

You have a responsibility to act and help others to take action.

Stop flitting between ideas and the latest get rich quick scheme. Dedicate your life to serving an issue that's important to you, others or the planet.

Be more David Attenborough.

CHAPTER 9
Don't roll over - lead and serve

As a marketer you're unique.

You have your own unique set of skills and knowledge. Use them and share them with the world.

It's your duty to serve and lead

You weren't put on this planet to take. You were put on this planet to share what you can with the world. Your purpose is to serve and you have a responsibility to do it.

You don't have a choice, it's your duty to serve.

If you see it as a choice, it'll be far too easy for you to give in. To be successful you need to do your time. You need to be ready to ride the hard waves and push through them when they seem impossible to overcome.

Running a business or being a marketer isn't for the faint hearted. At times you wonder why on earth you chose this life? But to be a successful marketer in uncertain times you need to be resilient, hard working and determined.

If you don't serve your audience, who else is going to? Maybe someone else will come along and pick up the task - but will they do it as well as you? Will they get the recognition for the idea you had? Will they be praised for the change they made?

Don't be the person who missed out on success because she couldn't be bothered. It's your duty to serve and lead your audience.

Serve doesn't mean lay down and rollover

When I use the term Serve I don't mean become a slave. The best leaders serve.

When I spoke to people about the idea behind this book, some people said "I don't want to be a servant." Well then this book isn't for you.

The best leaders, entrepreneurs and marketers have dedicated their lives to serving. They identify a need for someone to fill the role of leader and they do everything they can to stay there. Whether it's Anita Roddick founding The Body Shop, Ben Francis starting GymShark or Yvon Chouinard launching Patagonia.

They all felt passionate about something, launched a business around it and put in the time to serve the people who were also passionate about that something.

What does your audience need?

What does your team need?

What does the world need?

Being a leader is tough, people will have different opinions. Sometimes people will want to bring you down. It's your job to stay determined. You need grit to know when to dig your heels in and push on despite the negativity.

I'm not saying you should bury your head in the sand. You need to constantly listen to feedback, but only from the people that matter.

You're not here to please everyone. You're here to serve your chosen audience to help them solve their specific problems. If they don't like something, listen and tweak.

The most valuable asset you have as a great marketer is the ability to have a two way conversation with your customers using digital and traditional media.

But when you get negative feedback from people who don't matter - people who have their own self interest at heart or those who are just pure nasty. Ignore them. You need conviction to know when you're doing the right thing for your audience. You need to have the staying power to weather the onslaught of people ready to bring you down.

You're strong. Serve but don't roll over. Stand your ground when you need to and remember you're here to serve the people who care about what you care about.

Conserve your energy

Now when I say don't roll over, I'm not saying you have to go all Viking. Choose your battles. If you're going to be successful you need to know when to fight your battles and when you should conserve your energy.

Business and marketing is a tiring game. Your competition is constantly trying to get one over on you. You're trying to stay ahead. You're trying to innovate and find new ways to deliver a better customer experience.

To succeed you need to treat your business as if it's a marathon, not a hundred metre sprint.

Why a marathon?

I recently read a blog by Stephen Black which spoke about one man's experience working with marathon runners. He said "Your mind is constantly processing information regarding the route, weather, road surface, hydration, gels, pacing and other runners. You're also dealing with the internal struggle. The voice in your head constantly doubting your ability to complete the race, telling you to give up and stop."

If you're in business, you will face similar challenges. That voice in your head telling you you're not good enough, stop, give up. Like a marathon runner you need to pace yourself throughout the race to finish it despite those voices. You need the energy to push through those bad days.

Anger as a driver

Anger is a powerful driver in business and marketing.

From #MeToo, plastics, the lack of women in top roles and unethical marketing the list of things to be angry about is endless and sometimes anger is the biggest emotion to drive you forward.

Anger can make you determined to make a change. To do things how they should be, to do things ethically and properly. But use anger wisely or it will destroy you.

For years I was driven by anger. I was raped when I was 15. The anger that I felt from that event made me angry at authority, angry at myself, angry at the world and angry at pretty much everything. For years after that anger developed into anger at the behaviour of business people and the egos of those in positions of power.

That anger served me well in the early years of freelancing and starting my marketing agency. It drove me to make the right decisions, to do things properly and to never have to work for someone else to tell me what to do again.

But anger can have a negative effect. At times I would send heated emails to people, get worked up over a bullsh*t LinkedIn post and have regular meltdowns. The power of anger can be a blessing but often it can become unhealthy.

Don't let anger take over, use it positively.

Channel that anger into something more positive. Instead of focusing on the negatives of other people's actions, concentrate on why what you're doing is good. If you think back to the power of giving back with your marketing that I mentioned in the previous chapter, you'll know the powerful effect of generosity on your mental health.

Try to find a positive emotion that drives you and don't let anger take over your days. It could hold you back.

F*ck the snowflake haters

If you care about the wellbeing of others, you're called a snowflake. If you're concerned about how your words and the words of others can impact people, you're called a snowflake. If you think we should be doing more to save our planet, you're a snowflake.

We're not snowflakes, we're changemakers.

We want a different type of business, we want a different culture. We want a different world and there's nothing wrong with that. I think it's quite the opposite. Someone who is willing to stand up against the status quo and work to make a change is far from a snowflake. You're here to last, you're strong and you don't melt away from a bit of name calling.

That doesn't mean it's us and them. Millenials and Boomers have more in common than you might think. To be successful in life and business we need to listen, understand and influence others. Successful marketers try to see why some people might feel the way they do. A lack of self worth, an annoyance at a lack of achievement or a dislike of change might lead certain people to call others snowflakes.

Just because someone doesn't agree with the change you're trying to make with your marketing doesn't mean you should melt away like a snowflake. Stick around and carry on driving forward.

Change is hard

If you're just starting out in business or you're a marketer in an established industry you'll know how hard it can be to bring about the change needed to drive an idea forward.

Long established industries don't want to be disrupted. You're competing with people with deep pockets and lots of resources. You need to think creatively, especially if you're just starting out.

In his "Tipping Point" book, Malcolm Gladwell talks about how ideas spread. It's a complicated business with the need for different types of people, the ideal circumstances and timing and stickiness to make sure the idea is shareable and memorable.

If you're not getting anywhere with your idea, don't give up. Persevere.

It might be that the timing isn't right for people to stand up and listen to you. It might be that you need to find more Connectors (the people in a community who know lots of people and make introductions), Mavens (people who know a lot about your space, they are information collectors and love to pass on their learning) or Salespeople (the people who love to share your story, they want to tell others about you).

If your startup is changing consumer behaviour, you're going to have an even tougher job making change happen. Breaking habits and building new ones takes time, it can take up to 254 days for an individual to form a new habit. Imagine how many days it will take to change the habits of a much larger group.

Constantly develop yourself

You've probably heard it before, the biggest investment you can make is in yourself.

In an age of chatbots, AI and automation the most important thing anyone can do now is to be learning. To be developing your soft skills, become a better leader and communicator.

The biggest way to keep ahead of competitors is to constantly learn. Always have a book in your hand or blog on your Chrome tabs. Research shows that reading results in improvements in knowledge, memory performance, stress reduction and vocabulary.

However, perhaps the biggest reason to read is the expansion in your ideas and thoughts. Reading allows you to take on valuable information and keep it locked away for when you might need it. It allows you to find influences that inspire you and shape your own ideas. No idea is truly unique, and as long as you don't copy other people's ideas and do credit those who inspire you, it's not plagiarism.

The difference between those who are successful and those who aren't is a dedication to personal development and furthering themselves. Instead of binge watching The Crown on Netflix, they're reading a book or enrolling on a new course.

It's time to rethink "nobody likes a know it all."

Because marketers who know a lot about their subject are the go to in their field, they get asked for comments by the media, they get invited to the latest brand launches and they stand out from the rest of their peers. They're a fountain of knowledge and they serve others by passing on their learning and knowledge. They're trusted and respected because of the time they put into learning and passing on that learning to others. Now there's a difference between someone who has a lot of knowledge on a subject and an egocentric know it all. Don't be the latter.

Use your knowledge to help others to achieve, inspire them to take action and pass on your learning to help people improve their lives.

She's a triple threat

Ariana Grande is a triple threat. She can sing, dance and act. She's unstoppable.

For those of you who don't know what a triple threat is. Google defines a triple threat as "a person, especially a performer or sports player, who is proficient in three important skills within their particular field."

This is a little narrow for the purpose of this book. So, I'm extending it to include a marketer, entrepreneur or business owner. To succeed as a marketer with the rise of technology and globalisation you need to be more Ariana. You need to become a triple threat.

- What are your three unique skills?

- What can you give to the world?

- What are your talents?

By combining valuable skills into one person -   you - you're unstoppable. Can you design? Are you great at writing? Are you better than most at building social media engagement? Are you good at public speaking?

Focus on your biggest three skills and hone them to become a real triple threat to your competition. Your unique mix of skills and knowledge make you a valuable asset to yourself, your business and the audience you serve.

Become a triple threat.

CHAPTER 10
Build a brand the right way

The tide is turning on unethical business practices, the end of the 2010s was dominated by big ego founders being ousted, silly startup valuations being questioned and sustainability became a hot topic for every business.

Whether you're just starting up, you're established or you're a marketer in an existing business it's time to question what type of business you want to build.

Brands of the future won't be able to be unethical

Pressure from environmental groups and consumers are forcing brands to change and improve the way they look at their impact on the planet. Regulators have introduced new laws including GDPR to stop some unethical marketing practices.

Brands of the future won't survive if they're not ethical and sustainable. Audiences demand more transparency and authenticity and those that can't offer it will continue to lose sales and eventually die. It's happening already, people are boycotting Amazon (I am aware of the irony if that's where you bought this book from) and Sports Direct brands over their working conditions and tax avoidance. Into the 2020s and 30s consumers will apply more pressure and unethical practice will be further demonised.

Mintel's 2015 UK consumer report found that 76% of UK adults say that the ethical and sustainable credentials of their products and the reputation of companies or brands are important when making a buying decision.

Your brand can't afford to behave unethically.

What is an ethical business?

An ethical business considers how its actions affect the environment, people and animals. Truly ethical brands look at the effects of their product right from conception to manufacturing, distribution and the supply chain of the materials that go into making their product or services.

Considerations over product manufacturing location, worker pay and conditions, sustainable material choices and sales tactics are all important to an ethical business. Sometimes the sustainable and ethical choice will be more expensive, for example plastic and plastic-derived materials like polystyrene are usually the cheapest materials to use in manufacturing but their negative effect on the planet is huge.

Being ethical goes beyond corporate social responsibility, often a corporate exercise for a good PR story. Instead businesses must move to create a brand that serves people and the planet while turning a profit.

A tough ask? Perhaps for some, but you're forward thinking. You know that the only way to create a successful brand of the future is to behave responsibly and use ethics as a driver for change for good.

Purpose and profit can coexist

There are traditionally two camps in business, not for profit and profit but a new type of brand exists. A purpose driven profitable enterprise.

The list of purpose driven brands turning a profit expands daily with new entrants such as those producing sustainable alternatives to existing non planet friendly products, software companies democratising data and fashion brands focusing on reducing waste.

A 2018 Accenture study of 30,000 consumers in 35 countries, found 62 percent of consumers want companies to take a stand on issues such as sustainability, transparency and fair employment practices. Consumers are no longer making decisions based solely on product and price. They choose companies based on whether the brand purpose aligns with their beliefs and values. They reject brands that don't align, with one in five walking away from a brand because of a misalignment in purpose and values.

Putting purpose at the heart of a brand is a driver of profitability. In 2016, Unliver saw purpose driven, sustainable brands within its portfolio grow 50 percent faster than its other brands, whilst contributing to more than 60 percent of the company's growth.

The old thinking that CSR is an add on needs to be put aside, purpose needs to be embedded and used as a driver. Communicating your purpose is vital to the profitability and growth of your brand.

Capitalism isn't cool anymore

The tide is turning on greedy capitalism.

Defined as "an economic and political system in which a country's trade and industry are controlled by private owners for profit, rather than by the state," the brand of capitalism we're living in at the moment has gone a lot further than private owners making a profit, with stories of established brands mistreating workers in warehouses compared to Victorian workhouses and workers overseas dying so western consumers can have fast fashion on demand.

Despite being one of the most developed economies and a big advocate of capitalism, the UK is now the most unequal society in the EU according to a 2017 study by Oxford University Professor Danny Dorling. Trickle down economics doesn't work and the wealthy just keep on getting richer and the poor get poorer.

Capitalism as it exists today is broken and change needs to happen.

Capitalism is cold and uncaring. Version 2.0 is needed. As a marketer, startup or entrepreneur you're perfectly placed to affect change. You can make the choice to build a business with impact. It's our job as marketers and businesses to reduce that gap. Your workforce should be treated fairly and paid well. Profit should never be at the expense of others and the planet. The impact of your products and services should be positive, the profits you make should be reinvested into helping others whilst still rewarding yourself and those who have helped you achieve the success you enjoy.

Being ethical doesn't make you a communist

A criticism I hear of ethical brands or people who choose a sustainable life is "it's a bit worthy," "you're a communist," "you'll never be successful by putting others first."

But being ethical doesn't mean you're a communist, there is a balance to be had. Profit shouldn't be at the expense of others. It shouldn't have an effect on the health of others and the planet.

A new type of business person exists. One who craves a purpose, their very being is to serve. To find their purpose and drive it forward to make a positive change in the world. They weren't put on this planet to take, they were born to lead and serve those who need their help.

Ethical leaders put people before profit, their decisions aren't purely profit driven. They understand they need to make a profit to survive and thrive but they also understand that it's not everything. Their success is measured by both business growth and the impact they make. They combine personal success with the success of others.

Being nice in business doesn't make you a communist. It makes you a positive role model to others, one who inspires others to take action about the things you're passionate about. Be the driver of change and become an ethical business leader.

Chasing the lifestyle

If you scroll through Instagram you'll see the latest influencer posing in front of a Bentley wearing Hugo Boss and a gold Rolex. On Facebook you'll see targeted ads for get rich schemes and people selling training who have never run a successful business in their life.

On Linkedin we're bombarded with posts from people who've "made it" or in reality, faking it until they've made it.

From an early age we're taught that if we work hard enough we will achieve a lifestyle sold to us as a dream. An off the shelf list of items, products and brands we need in our life. Social media has amplified the pressure we feel as consumers to conform to social norms but it has always existed with the "Keeping up with the Joneses" mentality being a part of British culture for decades.

To build a business with impact you need to stop chasing the lifestyle and contributing to the unhealthy obsession we all have with status. Lifestyle is not enough to keep you going through the tough times in business. You need something bigger, because to create real change you're going to come up against a lot of obstacles. The promise of a Lamborghini or Rolex isn't enough. If you've followed the Define stage of this book, you should have identified that purpose. Use that instead of the promise of a pay off that might never come.

The Black Friday bloodbath

Black Friday 2019 fell on the last payday for most people before Christmas, meaning retailers tried to outcompete each other to not lose market share. Barclaycard said transaction volumes were up 12.5% from 2018.

In a drive to the bottom, some retailers cut prices by 75 percent. Discounting might drive short term sales but it doesn't drive long term value to anyone. It creates waste, reduces profits and decreases brand loyalty. In a glimmer of hope for us all and the planet, some forward thinking brands closed shop and decided not to participate.

Removing the ego from business

The 2010s were the year we started to care about the way startups behave. Fyre Festival and WeWork were just two of the big stories that dominated the business and startup headlines.

Businesses are now being put under a microscope, their inner workings and behaviour exposed and questionable behaviour called out.

Adam Neumann was ousted from WeWork and rightfully so. Charismatic leaders like Adam have pulled the wool over people's eyes for far too long, including juggernauts like SoftBank who have also been accused of deliberately overhyping valuations for their own benefit.

Questionable behaviour is ignored, private jets are purchased and one day it all comes crashing down leaving the employees and investors to pick up the pieces whilst the founder walks off with $1.7billion after nearly killing your company off.

People put startup founders on a pedestal and are quick to back the entrepreneur putting up money and their trust. Startups are lauded for their flat structures yet founders aren't accountable to their employees or business. Because they came up with a great idea and built a business, they're heroes. Wrong. Egos need to be clipped back sometimes and questionable behaviour should be questioned.

Fyre Festival is a similar story. A charismatic leader or a fraud, whichever way you want to look at it, came up with an idea and investors, employees and customers bought into the hype. The ego of the leader drives the idea forward to the point of no return. In the end, Billy McFarland was sent to prison for 6 years. A suitable end for a fraud.

Ego kills businesses and if you want to build a successful brand you need to keep your ego and those of other leaders in your business in check. It's easy to get carried away with early success and lose sight of your purpose to serve your audience.

Don't be an Adam or a Billy. Keep your ego in check.

Finding a sustainable business model

Successful startups don't chase the money from day one, they focus on building a solid group of raving fans. By truly understanding the needs of their customers and audience, they're able to build products and services that provide enormous value, something people are willing to pay for.

All brands need money to survive. Charities need donations, businesses need profits. In order to serve your audience, you're going to need a sustainable business model by identifying the problems your audience is willing to pay to fix.

Some ethical founders and marketers struggle with pricing, you need to find a place for your product or service between giving it away, making a healthy profit, and greed. There needs to be profit in what you're doing, otherwise the business will fail and any work you've done to date will be for nothing.

You will never achieve your purpose if you don't turn a profit. Profit allows you to reinvest and make positive change.

Culture affects your brand

Brands can become obsessed with growth and hitting revenue goals.

Former Revolut employees exposed a toxic culture of unpaid work, unachievable targets, and high-staff turnover in the fintech startup. It raises questions about the growth at all costs model employed by many organisations.

Whilst growth is important to realise business objectives and impact against a purpose there needs to be a balance. Sports Direct is another example of putting profit before ethical growth. Working conditions in their distribution centres has been widely reported with a strike system and culture of fear that speaking out will lose employees their jobs.

Startups have relied on culture tricks like slides and breakout spaces for too long as a way to disguise the hostile environments commonplace in lots of businesses.

Eventually internal cultures become tangled up with the brand and your audience's perception of the brand. Creating a positive culture should be an important consideration for every brand, not just startups. All brands need to attract talent and customers to thrive. Bad cultures can negatively affect both.

Taking culture seriously and creating one that breeds creativity, positivity and innovation is key to growing an ethical brand that stands the test of time. As a marketer or entrepreneur you have an influence on the culture within your organisation. You have a choice between a happy culture based around shared values or a culture of growth at any expense.

Making time to serve

When you change your mindset to serve rather than take, you automatically put your audience's needs before your own. Value driven relationships are the bedrock of every strong brand and help build strong connections that stand the test of time. By existing you're already serving but take it one stop further and make time for non paid work.

Hold Q&A sessions on social media to give away your knowledge, volunteer a certain percentage of your working month, give away premium content instead of gating it with forms. Find ways you can serve your audience that deliver real value.

The more you give the more you receive. This isn't why you do it of course but the pay off when you commit to serving your audience is huge. From increased brand trust to loyal fans who help promote your cause to their closest friends, family and colleagues. Something I'm sure you'll agree is extremely valuable whatever stage your business is at.

It's time to decide what sort of business you want to build. Is it a cold, heatless brand nobody loves? Or is it a business that's passionate about the causes its audience cares about? One that delivers real change and has a positive impact on others and the planet.

Build a business with impact.

CHAPTER 11
Your audience needs to take centre stage

Consumers and buyers have more power than ever with more information than they know what to do with. Consumers are slowing gaining more power especially over their own data and permission.

Don't just watch the sea change happen, be a driver of it. Do everything you can to empower your audience by being more transparent and authentic. Treat their data carefully. Be honest when things go wrong and be open with your customers. They will respect you for your honesty and integrity.

Not only are you building a more meaningful relationship with your customers, you're helping to reshape the marketing industry to become more trusted.

Give your audience the information they need

As a responsible marketer you have a duty to ensure your audience has all the information they need to make informed buying decisions. That means you need to present information in a digestible way your potential customers can understand at every stage of their buying journey.

Give them ways to solve their problems themselves at the awareness stage. At the consideration stage give them all the facts about your product or service. Provide a real comparison to your competition at the purchase stage make sure your contracts are clear and don't hold any nasty surprises.

The best marketers don't try to oversell and underdeliver, they provide all the information to give their audience a transparent, realistic look at how the brand works.

If you're not the best fit for a prospect or customer, be honest and recommend someone else. The damage that can be done to your brand by onboarding wrong fit customers can be huge. The reputational damage that can be done by providing services and products that aren't a right fit can be catastrophic too.

Be ethical and share the information your audience needs.

Listen to your audience

No matter what industry you're in you have access to feedback. Technology platforms get reviews on Capterra, food businesses get reviews on TripAdvisor and ecommerce brands get social media comments from satisfied as well as dissatisfied customers daily.

We live in an age in which it has never been easier to get it right in business, yet businesses continue to ignore valuable free marketing help. Businesses before the internet age didn't have access to this valuable marketing information, they'd only know customers weren't happy when they stopped buying.

The best marketers are great listeners. They take on board the learning from reviews, they read between the lines to find ways to improve their offering and listen to feedback to allow them to grow.

You have a wealth of free information about what works and doesn't work in your organisation right in front of you. Use it to improve your brand and better serve your audience.

You need your customers to love you

Customer churn is one of the biggest wastes of resource in business. There will of course be a natural churn depending on your industry, in B2B industries for example some of your customers will go out of business.

But in most businesses, customer churn and the need to constantly find new customers can be stopped.

Research in 2013 by Harvard Business Review found 68% of customers said they had left a brand because they felt it was indifferent toward them. By serving your audience consistently you have the opportunity to stop that 68% of customers from leaving. To make someone feel appreciated and looked after is a simple step most businesses can take with an effective communication strategy.

It's hard to believe that most companies don't invest in existing customer relationship building with the same Harvard Business Review research finding 91% of small businesses doing nothing to retain their existing clients, despite companies that prioritise customer experience generate 60% higher profits than their competition.

If you want to stay in business for a sustained period to deliver the impact you set out to make, you need to invest in building stronger connections with your existing customers and help them to fall in love with your brand.

Create a customer experience strategy

Going further than customer service, customer experience (CX) is the sum of interactions between you and your audience. They include interactions at every stage of the customer's journey with a brand from awareness, consideration, purchase, after care and loyalty.

Just like a successful brand having a vision, you need a clear vision for your customer experience. Like the Serve Marketing Manifesto to guide ethical marketing (at the back of this book), you should have a set of guiding principles to follow to deliver a consistent customer experience. This vision will set out the way you will interact with and speak to customers.

Customer experience isn't just for physical interactions. Successful marketers think about how their audience might think and feel at every stage of their buying journey. Ecommerce brands could use video chat to match products to consumers, B2B brands might focus on training teams to build better relationships with clients, all of which can build a better customer experience.

To create a customer experience strategy, first focus on identifying all of the touchpoints and interactions your audience has with your brand during their journey. How do you want your customer feel at each point of contact? How can you make their experience 1% better? If you improved 100 touchpoints by 1% you'd improve your customer experience by 100%.

It's likely your touchpoints are going to be across different channels, making sure the experience is consistent across all social media.

Constantly monitor the experience against your ideal customer experience. If you're not living up to the vision you've set out in your strategy, work out why not and fix it. Sustained delivery of a consistent customer experience builds an army of engaged, loyal customers.

Meet your audience

In a digital world it's easy to hide behind our screens, firing off Instagram DMs and emails has become the norm. But nothing will ever be a more effective driver of change in your business than meeting your audience face to face and hearing words direct from your customers' mouths.

There's a reason why top branding and marketing agencies hold focus groups and customer interviews as part of a new client onboarding process. They want to get to the real root of the good and bad of an organisation, to shape and build a marketing strategy to better satisfy an audience.

If you have customers, great. Pick up the phone or send an email inviting them to have a chat. Hold an informal workshop to find out their problems and see how well you're helping them to solve them.

If you don't have customers, talk to people interested in the space you're in. Connect with like-minded people who are part of your target audience on social media in your city. Go for a coffee with them, ask them questions about their dreams, goals and problems. You'll be surprised how open people are.

The information you get from meeting your audience face to face is invaluable and technology has yet to invent a better alternative.

Brands don't control the conversation anymore

For years brands would push out expensive advertising campaigns and shape public opinion of their brand with little chance of them being held to account over the promises they made.

Now, brands are being held to account. Big news stories like VW diesel scandal and the UKFast CEO sexual assault allegations shine a light on the practices that go on behind closed doors that brands would rather we didn't know about. The stories that years ago would have likely been buried by a shiny advertising campaign are now here to stay with social media amplifying the stories.

In recent years, bad news stories and pressure from consumers around issues like palm oil, plastics and CEO behaviour has led to changes in consumer behaviour and buying decisions. Companies can no longer send out press releases or brainwash the masses, consumers demand real action and change. Your audience now controls the conversation around important topics like sustainability and company culture.

Empowering customers has been great for brands who behave ethically and take care of the planet in particular. UK consumers are turning their backs on unethical businesses, the 2018 Ethical Consumer Markets Report found 49% of under 24s avoided a product or service because of its negative environmental impact in the last year.

You can't control the way your audience talk about your brand and rightfully so. As consumers we demand more from the businesses we choose to work with and the number of people making buying decisions based on ethics and values is increasingly rapidly.

With all of the benefits of increased consumer information and power, comes less brand control which can be challenging for businesses when communicating across so many different channels. That's why communication strategy is so important, you can't frame the way others talk about your brand but you can frame the way they think about your brand. Giving you more chance of your message coming across in the way you intend.

A lack of clear communication could mean a blurring of your purpose and message, resulting in chinese whispers. You push one message on your social media channels, your website messaging is different and the way you write your emails is different again, all leading to a game of Chinese whispers where your brand message gets confused, making it harder for your customers and network to communicate what you do to others.

By simplifying your communications to become consistent and shareable you give your audience the opportunity to share a succinct, impactful message to others in their network.

Customer success is the best marketing tool you have

The easiest way to succeed in business? Invest in delivering the best customer experience and ensure every interaction with your business is successful.

Customer success is the process of anticipating customer challenges and overcoming them before they arise to ensure their needs are met effectively. Customer success increases customer loyalty, happiness and lifetime value.

Often only utilised in B2B software companies, customer success is a marketing strategy every brand can take advantage of. With rising customer acquisition costs affecting profitability, by better serving the needs of your audience you can reduce the need for new customer acquisition and build a base of loyal fans of your brand.

To use it effectively, you need to define what customer success looks like in your organisation. Is it how your brands makes a customer feel when they've purchased? Is it the change in state? Does it solve a specific problem that results in a feeling of happiness?

B2B brands might focus on education as part of their customer success programme, creating a department of account managers to answer and solve any questions your customers might have. A B2C brand might look at product design and customer service in their customer success strategy to better anticipate and communicate how a product should be used to achieve the best result for the customer.

As with any branding and marketing initiative, it is important to measure customer success with objectives put in place to check customer complaints, satisfaction and loyalty.

Create a customer success strategy

Again, your customer success strategy will vary depending on the type of business you're in and what your customers expect from you but there are some steps you can follow to create a strategy for your brand:

1. **Identify your customers' goals**: why are they purchasing your product or service? What do they want to achieve or feel when they've gone through the buying journey?

2. **Decide who is going to be responsible for customer success:** if you're a startup or small business you might take on the role of customer success manager. If you're in a larger team, customer service and marketing teams should work together to decide who is going to form your customer success team.

3. **Communicate what customer success looks like at every stage of the buying journey to the appropriate team:** a roadmap should be created to ensure whatever has been defined as customer success is met. Everyone in the team should know what is expected of them to ensure the needs of the customer are met.

4. **Set objectives and measure as you go:** is your customer happy? Are they getting the value they need from your product or service? If not, where is your strategy falling down? Identify improvements in your strategy and implement changes.

The power of user generated content

Millenials hate being sold to, they want to make their own journey through a purchasing process. Strong independent females ain't got time for sales people either. But in all seriousness, the key to selling to the biggest buying demographic is to show not tell.

How? User generated content.

What is user generated content (UGC)? It's pretty self explanatory. UGC is content generated by your users, audience or customers. It comes in many formats from reviews, videos, blogs and images just to name a few.

Resharing content with the permission of the creator helps build trust and show others in your audience how much your customers love you and how they're using your brand in their lives.

You can use UGC across different channels in written or visual format but perhaps the best way to use audiences content is with photos on your social media platforms. User generated photos are 5x more likely to convert customers versus non user generated content. It's a no brainer.

If you're an ecommerce brand you'll likely have lots of product shots on your website, that's great but your audience want to see your product in real life situations before they decide to buy. UGC is like a constant photoshoot of your products in real life situations.

User generated content is also a form of social proof. Social proof works because people see people like them making the same decision. Since so many other people behave in that way or buy this product, it must be the correct behavior. Social proof like UGC speeds up the decision stage of a customer buying journey.

Use UGC at different stages of your customer journey to add value. At the awareness stage you can use your users images in your social posts to show your products, at the consideration stage you could use reviews or unboxing videos and at the loyalty stage you could use 'how to' videos or tutorial content generated by your audience to educate others on how to get the most out of your product or service.

The final benefit of UGC is the invaluable feedback you can get. Everytime someone in your audience shares, tags or reviews your brand, it's a step towards a stronger brand. Positive posts and reviews are a visible vote for you brand. Negative reviews can be used to improve your business and give you an opportunity to respond respectfully and empathetically, backing up your credentials as an ethical brand that serves its customers and takes feedback on board to improve.

You need to start identifying ways to get your hands on more user generated content in your communications strategy.

Give your audience the tools they need to communicate your message

We've talked about how to use user generated content but how do you give your audience the tools they need to help communicate your message.

First of all, ask.

If you don't ask, you won't get. If you've done the work to establish yourself as a brand who cares about your audience and done your time to serve your audience you'll have the trust of your customers.

Ask them for product reviews by sending them review links. Big review platforms like reviews.co.uk and TrustPilot are a great way to start building a bank of reviews you can use in your marketing communications.

Ask customers to post on social media platforms like Instagram with branded hashtags. In previous chapters we discussed the benefit of giving back, the same physiological principles apply here. Your customers want to give back too. They want to pass on good experiences with brands to people in their network.

Another way to generate content from your users is giveaways. Giveaways are a good way to generate content quickly, by asking your followers on social media to submit content in return entering them into a giveaway of your products.

Branded assets are another way to help your customers spread your message. Branded social media content, downloadable PDF content and blogs are a few ways you can give your audience content to share with others who might be interested in what you're up to. The focus as with all of your content should be on adding value to your audience and creating something that doesn't sell directly, branded content should be there to educate, entertain or inspire.

Make your customers the centre of your communications strategy, they're the real stars of the show, and the reason you went into business in the first place - to serve them and solve their problems.

Focus on creating a shareable experiences

If you've read any of the previous chapters, you'll know I'm not a fan of the WeWork brand.

But one thing they do well is to keep on brand whilst personalising their approach depending on the location of the space. Trying to tie themselves to the style and unique culture within locations they personalise the decor and theming of the space to tap into existing design themes in the city. It all helps to communicate a message of personalisation.

There's a reason why the best restaurants have unique entrances or plating techniques. They've created "Instagrammable" brands. These all form part of the branding and marketing strategy of the business. They are a way to communicate with diners and potential customers by creating a unique, shareable experience.

The best places don't always win, the most shareable venues do. They catch on and become the "go to place" because everyone is talking about them.

You can utilise similar tactics in your business too.

- What can you do to make your brand experience more memorable?

- What can you do to make your customers want to tell everyone they see today about you?

- What can you do to make your brand shareable?

A 2010 study by the University of Pennsylvania showed that content that evokes emotion is more likely to be shared. The same goes for experiences, tap into emotion to create a shareable experience and you will set your brand up for success.

The best brands put their customers centre stage and give them an experience to remember. Your audience love telling stories. By serving up an unforgettable brand experience with a shareable message you're using your number one growth tool. Your audience.

CHAPTER 12
Building an unbeatable brand toolkit

Naming, tone of voice, logos, values and behaviours, signage, marketing material, websites and communication documents are all part of your brand.

Bringing them all together is the hard part. With multiple platforms and uses each element of your brand is a puzzle piece ready to be put together to create one clear image to your audience. Your brand toolkit is your complete jigsaw. Your weapons room of effective tools to connect with your audience in a meaningful way.

Your toolkit allows you to be unique, to stand out and represent yourself to your audience, you're their leader and you need to make sure that comes across in every single communication you have with them.

Digestible messaging

Whatever format they come in, communications are essentially messages. You need to use language and design that your audience understands. Keep jargon and BS terms away from your brand and speak in the language your audience uses but stay authentic.

KFC is a prime example of understanding your audience. Their advertising and messaging has evolved over the years to stay current, their "What the cluck?" campaign was banned by the advertising standards authority for causing offence. Causes offence to who? Those who it wasn't intended to reach. The demographic and audience the campaign was aimed at got it. And that's all KFC needed.

In order to get a message across sometimes you have to alienate groups who aren't in your audience. Remember back in chapter five I said it's good if not everyone gets what you do, this is why.

Be authentic to your brand and use messaging your audience connects with, forget about those outside of your audience. It's not for them.

Perform a communication audit

Communications planning can be complex and time consuming, but without a plan in place your communications strategy is going to fall flat.

Before you start designing social headers, adverts and websites first map out all of the possible communications you're likely to make as a brand.

What channels are you going to communicate on? Will they be a mix of offline or online? What documents do you or your sales team need? What do your communications look like currently? Do they need updating?

Give your brand the tools it needs to serve your audience.

Your communications audit should bring together every single piece of literature and messaging you've sent out in the last 6 months. By putting all your content in one place you'll soon see inconsistencies and areas for improvement.

Is the message consistent across all of the communications? Are you using the same tone of voice and language? Does imagery look consistent across all of the documents?

This might take some time but it's a worthwhile exercise to ensure your brand is consistent online and offline. There is nothing worse to its audience than a brand that says and does different things, it's a sure fire way to lose trust and loyalty.

Template your communication

If someone joined your friendship group and spoke differently every time you spoke to them you'd probably start hearing alarm bells in your head. The same goes for your brand, if you're not communicating consistently with the same tone of voice and personality, your audience is going to start to lose trust in you.

The easiest easy way to produce on brand content every time is to template your communications. Have set processes and templates in place for different types of communications.

If you're running a social advertisement, have a template in place that tells whoever is designing the ad where brand assets should be placed. Have content writing templates in place. Have a best practice example of each document to compare against once you've produced new material.

Visual document templates like poster design templates are great for saving time and being consistent. Having logos and formatting already templated within a document means one less chance for inconsistency.

If you haven't already got brand guidelines, start working on them. Consistency is key to an impactful message. Depending on your role, you'll likely be working with people outside of your brand whether it's news publications, designers or web developers. Your guidelines are a set of rules for everyone who uses your brand to abide by, they allow you to protect your brand and keep it consistent wherever it's used.

Take guidelines one step further and produce a brand manual, top brands like Nike use brand manuals to onboard new employees and suppliers to make sure they live and breathe the brand.

Consistent digital & print communications

Digital and print might be two completely different communication mediums but consistency is still key.

Things like colours will need to be tailored for on screen and print use, not all colours work well in print and not all colours can be shown on mobile devices because of screen capability and limited colour palettes.

A lot of brands struggle with bridging the gap between digital and print but it's an essential job as a marketer. You need your audience to get your message and know it's your brand communication straight away, whether they're seeing it digitally or offline.

The power of design

Design says a lot about your brand. Effective design not only makes communication easier, it also builds trust. When your audience sees you have invested in design, they feel a sense of encouragement and trust that you're a progressive brand.

Great design is at the heart of every successful brand. From product design to user experience design and graphic design. Brands like Adobe and Apple have centred their businesses around the power of design.

Design thinking makes communicating easier. Dieter Rams' famous quote says *"Good design is as little design as possible."* He's not wrong. Most brands over complicate design and forget what it's there to do. Design is a communication tool.

The fonts, colours and imagery you use communicate an image. Use design as part of your toolkit to deliver impactful messages with less words.

What are your moments of truth?

What is a moment of truth?

Capturing your audience's attention is vital to the success of your brand. How long do you have to make an impact? This is an example of a moment of truth. You need to give your audience a reason to stick around in that moment or you've lost an opportunity to start a meaningful conversation with a potential customer.

Aftersales is often treated as an upsell opportunity in business - what else can we flog you while we've got your attention - but it's often forgotten as part of a communication strategy.

Aftersales is a huge missed opportunity for marketers.

One of your jobs as a marketer is to create positive brand experiences and ensure a buyer gets what they need from a transaction with your brand. Keeping a check on moments of truth like after a sale has been made is an easy way to make sure you have your finger on the pulse of how well you're meeting the needs of your customers.

I'm sure you've heard of buyers remorse. You might have had it when you've purchased an item and regretted it. You need to understand why someone might get buyers remorse, is it maybe because they don't know what to do with the product or service? Can you give them some help to get the most value out of it?

Every brand has different moments of truth, what are they in your business? How can you develop them to keep your audience's attention and serve their needs?

Embed and evolve

As you go through your 20s into your 30s, sometimes your priorities change. Life happens and your views adapt. This will happen with your audience, to thrive you need to embed your brand in your chosen market and evolve as they did.

Your toolkit should constantly evolve as your audience does. If they start to use a new platform, decide if you should adopt it and tailor your messaging to its new home. When you embed yourself in an audience it's easier to anticipate changes in behaviour, constantly assess your messaging to check its still relevant and impactful.

Customer service is part of your toolkit

When we think about customer service, we usually think of call centres and people sat managing social media support handles on Twitter.

Customer service interactions are also part of your communication plan. How do you speak to your customers? How do you respond to queries on social media? The way we respond to feedback and questions tells your audience a lot about what sort of brand you are, it forms part of your brand toolkit. A way of showing your customers who you are.

When something goes wrong, it's okay, nobody is perfect. However, marketing and the business as a whole needs to take responsibility and learn from mistakes.

Successful marketers take responsibility for delivering on the brand's promise from start to finish of a customer journey. Marketers must take responsibility and make sure all customer touchpoints match with ethics and deliver on their audience's expectations by being responsive and proactive.

Being honest with your brand

Consumers are more trusting of brands that are open and honest. Consumers like brands with personality, ones they can connect with on a meaningful level. By being honest about where you're at, you seem more human.

At an event recently I heard about one sustainable cosmetics company's struggle to find a non plastic alternative to its shampoo bottles, they had tried cardboard but it kept disintegrating and other environmentally friendly options just weren't feasible for their size of business at the moment. By being honest and sharing the process of trying to find and test alternatives, people are much more forgiving and buy into the journey the brand is on towards achieving their purpose.

Two of the biggest weapons in your brand toolkit should be honesty and transparency. They're extremely valuable assets.

The power of repetition

At the time of writing this book, it is election season in the UK. Tag lines are in full swing and the party lines are being wheeled out like the karaoke machine at Christmas.

Why do they do it? It's often said in marketing that someone must see or hear a message 7 times before it sinks in. That's 7 times of hearing the dreaded meaningless election taglines before they get stuck in your head.

Whilst it might be annoying and frustrating, repetition and frequency of messaging are important in communications. Sending out one email or social media post isn't going to land your message. You need to use repetition.

Having said that, it's important to know when enough is enough. Having an armoury of messages and ways to communicate is essential, but move away from taglines and move towards a diverse brand toolkit.

The easiest way to communicate with your audience is to live your brand purpose, as every decision and action your organisation takes sends a message to your audience. Make sure that message aligns with your brand, its reason for existing and your audience.

Section 3: Amplify
Amplify the effects of your work
tactics, partnerships, marketing

Resource: Continuous Marketing Improvement Loop

The Continuous Marketing Improvement Loop is explained in more detail in the next chapter but here's a copy to use in your marketing planning.

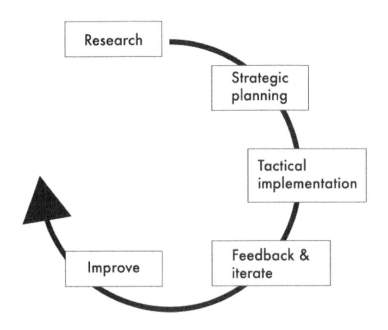

CHAPTER 13
Continuous marketing improvement

Marketing isn't a one time activity, it needs to be a constant in your brand to succeed. It's not a set and forget type job, you need to constantly renew your marketing to stay relevant.

I mentioned in the previous chapter that marketing, despite common thinking, isn't just a promotional tool. It's essentially the bridge between your organisation and your customers. It's your vehicle to reach the audience you've chosen to serve and deliver the value you have promised.

Standing still in marketing isn't possible in today's world. To succeed you need to adopt continuous marketing improvement. The term continuous improvement can be traced back to the Japanese term "kaizen" which means change for the better.

Kaizen first came about in Japan after the Second World War. In manufacturing the continuous improvement concept helped Toyota to become the largest car manufacturer on the planet.

So what has Toyota's success got to do with marketing? Continuous improvement can be applied to marketing too. The idea that every process in an organisation can be improved to generate more value for a customer whilst reducing waste is a concept that should be adopted by marketing departments in all organisations.

Marketing teams should be on a mission to constantly develop and improve themselves, striving for the perfection of processes to better serve the customer. For example, combining user behavioural data with your customer email marketing database could improve the marketing messages you serve your prospects, in turn improving campaign response rates and reducing resource wastage in the form of less email unsubscribers.

Continuous marketing improvement is needed in fast developing markets and gives forward thinking companies an edge over their competitors.

Marketing improvement is good for everyone

Improving marketing isn't just great for your organisation, it's great for your audience too. It enables you to better serve their needs by continuously improving on every aspect of marketing from product to promotion.

You become better at meeting and anticipating your audience's needs: Using lean principles by testing your messaging and content you better understand the needs of your audience, putting you in a stronger position to meet and exceed them.

You build more meaningful relationships with your audience: By focusing on marketing that adds value by constantly evolving to be better connected to your audience, you're able to build deeper connections based on trust and mutual respect.

Reduce marketing spend wastage: Marketing budgets are valuable. Every penny spent should be to better serve your audience, by wasting marketing spending on tactics that don't work you're wasting valuable money that could be spent improving your customer experience.

The Continuous Marketing Improvement Loop

Marketing teams should be using continuous marketing improvement but how would you implement it in your organisation? By using the Continuous Marketing Improvement Loop to develop a consistent process of marketing improvement.

Research, Strategic Planning, Tactical Implementation, Feedback, Improve.

Research: Before you start any marketing campaign you should always understand your audience, your competitors, your product's strengths and weaknesses and your value proposition. In a continuous marketing improvement loop, the research stage helps deliver new insights into your market at the start of each campaign.

Strategic planning: If you've read any of this book you'll know how important strategy is, without strategy your tactics will fall flat. A clearly defined strategy is essential to the success of your marketing campaigns. At the strategic planning stage you should be asking questions:

- What are the reasons we want to launch this campaign and what do we want to achieve?

- Who are we targeting?

- What pains or motivations do our audience have?

- How will this campaign help them solve their problems?

- What are the core themes and messages in this campaign?

Using the answers to these questions you can start to build a campaign around your audience, offering value and producing a campaign that helps them address their problems. Marketing campaigns focused on helping potential customers are more effective than those pushing for a sale.

Tactical implementation: Using the information you collected in the Research and Strategic Planning phases of the improvement loop it's time to implement your learnings. The best campaign results are achieved when you test tactics. You can use previous campaign metrics to measure how effective tactics have been in the past but without trying them it's hard to know how effective they will be.

Different messages are best delivered using different tactics. For example, content marketing campaigns could use a mix of written and video content across your website and social media profiles.

Testing which tactics have the best response rate is important. Before perfecting each tactic use the minimum viable product (MVP) and tweak accordingly to minimise wasted time and resources on unsuccessful ideas.

Feedback & iterate: Usually feedback is left until the end of a marketing campaign, but it's essential to build regular feedback intervals into your marketing initiatives to measure the effectiveness of your strategy and tactics as you go along.

Website and social media data is great at the feedback stage. Information on bounce rates, social shares and comments are all vital to help you assess how well your campaign is doing. Measure the performance of each tactic to decide which should be improved, dropped or pushed harder. By doing more of what works and less of what doesn't you're utilising the lean principles that work for other successful brands.

Improve: At the end of your campaign you should collate all of the information you've gathered from it into a format that's easy to measure. Translate the information you have on effective messaging, tactics and strategy into improvement points.

- Which channels worked well?

- Where did messaging fall flat?

- What content resonated with our audience?

- What would we change with our personas, messaging and channels to better serve our audience in our next campaign?

Using an improvement loop approach to your marketing allows you to keep up with the evolving needs of your audience. Technology changes rapidly and social and search algorithms can change within the duration of a campaign - using constant feedback and iteration helps you to stay on top of those changes to deliver value to your audience and meet the objectives you set.

Adapting to different stages in your brand life cycle

Every brand is at a different stage, identify where you and your brand are within the brand life cycle.

Product & service development: You have an idea, you know what problems you're going to solve. This stage is about the design, production and research carried out to develop products and services to solve those audience problems. Marketing should be used at this stage to research trends, communicate with your audience and use data to identify opportunities. Market research and social listening are both marketing strategies that should be used to develop a better offering.

Introduction: Using an MVP (minimum viable product) model, brands will launch their new products or services in beta to test response to them. By handing over your offering before it's 100% finished you can gain valuable marketing feedback to improve. The product and service development stage is never really over for forward thinking brands and should form part of an innovation strategy. During the introduction stage, marketing campaigns are launched to grow brand awareness and build a base of engaged customers actively using the brand's products and services. Building email marketing lists and social followers is key at the introduction stage to grow a group of engaged product testers and early adopters.

Growth: Your brand has gained a small base of customers and is gaining momentum, market share is growing but more competition is entering the market or copying your offering. Customer acquisition is the main goal at growth stage. Marketing is needed not only to win new customers quickly but also to highlight the value of your product or service over that of your rival brands. Direct response marketing, advertising and content marketing are all tools you can utilise at the growth stage to win new customers.

Maturity: Successful brands will reach maturity stage with a sizable chunk of their market. Sales are starting to plateau and growth slows. At this stage, brands might look to add new products or services to continue growth or consolidate their position in the market using brand marketing. Display advertising might be one brand marketing tactic you would use at maturity.

Decline: Unfortunately, decline happens to most brands. You're at the top of the market with a big market share but sales are starting to fall. Customer behaviour or market trends are both reasons for falling sales and often result in the need to reduce prices or develop new products. At decline you should revert back to the strategies you used in the introduction phase to understand why sales are declining and identify new opportunities to serve your audience.

The purpose of covering the different stages of a brand's life cycle is to demonstrate that different stages require different approaches. By understanding where your brand is currently you can better assess what type of marketing is needed to get you to the next stage or maintain your position.

Seth Godin talks about how small brands shouldn't use brand marketing and focus purely on direct marketing. I'm a believer in balance. Without a strong brand, you may struggle to convert customers at the growth stage. A combination of brand and direct marketing, with varying focus between the two at different stages, is a great approach.

Outcome guides everything

Whatever your approach to marketing you should always be focused on the outcome for your brand and audience. What do you want the outcomes of your marketing campaign to be? Keep these in mind whenever you're writing marketing plans.

When you're focused on the outcome you become laser focused on what you need to do to achieve that outcome. Your only focus is on delivering value to your audience and your brand. Once you've identified your outcome, you need a marketing strategy to get there. Don't flit between strategies, your strategy is your map showing how you're going to get to your desired outcome.

Every marketing campaign is an experiment. You don't know if it's going to work or if it's going to be a flop. The only two non variables in this experiment are your outcomes and your strategy. Swap, change, iterate, alter and test your tactics but keep your constants. If you have a clear strategy in place you should be able to select the best tactics to deliver the most impact.

What do you want to achieve? Select the tactics based on strategy.

Use an owned, earned and paid ratio to make it a little easier to select tactics to support your strategy. Owned media are the communication channels you have within your control, they might be your website, blog or email marketing list. Paid media is basically anything you pay for, both social and traditional advertising fall into this category. Earned media is publicity gained through promotional efforts other than paid media advertising, these could be reviews, social shares or brand mentions.

Test ratios of owned, earned and paid media splits in your campaigns. Marketing campaigns should successfully blend all three to create a balanced campaign combining different media types to build awareness and trust. Finding the right ratio in your brand is important to build a blended marketing communication strategy. A ratio of 3:2:1 - 3 parts owned, 2 parts earned, 1 part paid - might work well for a B2B brand with a smaller marketing budget. A 1:2:3 ratio might work better for an FMCG brand with deeper pockets.

Shorter term thinking

In today's fast-paced, ever changing business world, marketers don't have the luxury of time to spend months working on campaigns based on a marketing plan drafted a year ago. This is why defining your chosen audience is so important, you must react and adapt to their changing needs.

Create a fluid marketing plan whilst maintaining focus on your long term marketing goals. You should never lose sight of your long term strategy, this is the driver of everything you do and flitting from strategy to strategy will result in poor performance and confused customers. Use long term strategic focus and short term campaigns.

Move towards shorter term campaign planning with a focus on producing responsive campaigns that can react to events and news. Responsive marketing like this can be more creative and iterative, both key characteristics of continuous improvement in marketing.

An easy way to execute regular campaigns is to use event based marketing, with the obvious route being to focus on seasonal events.

Christmas and Valentines are two prime examples. But marketing during these times is more expensive and competitive. Your brand will get caught in a lot of noise and crossfire from other brands. If you do choose to include popular events in your campaign planning, make sure you're doing something different. Don't use red hearts and a hideous script font for Valentines. Be unique. Be you.

Instead of being like everybody else, focus on producing theme based campaigns. What themes could you use for campaigns? What dates are important to your audience. International Women's Day could form the basis of one campaign. Earth Day might form another month long campaign. Whatever dates you choose, theme your campaigns around them and drive a clear message throughout.

Responsive, real time marketing

An easy way to gain exposure is to respond to topical events and news stories. Super Bowl reactions are just as big as Super Bowl ads.

Ikea's Balenciaga bags, McDonalds' turning their M upside down for International Women's Day Campaign, Nando's cheeky reference to the Spotify Wrapped campaign and those Jacob Rees-Mogg IKEA memes are all examples of how you can use real time marketing to respond to events. Each of these campaigns won tonnes of earned media in the form of social shares, media coverage and comments.

Clever real time campaigns are the backbone of some of our favourite brands and should be a part of your strategy too. Thinking creatively about a response to a real time event can grow your brand awareness exponentially, just make sure your real time marketing is on brand.

Setting a marketing budget

Marketing is the biggest driver of a business yet it has one of the most dispensable budgets. Company sales slow, marketing spending is reduced. A recession hits, marketing spending is cut. Why? Surely when others are cutting spending it's our opportunity to attack and win new customers. When company sales are down, surely we should be investing in marketing to find out why they're slowing and try to reverse the backwards slide.

To decide on marketing budgets, many businesses allocate a percentage of revenues to marketing. Small business marketing budgets range from 3-10% of revenue but marketing budget allocation is usually dependant on factors like your industry, the pace at which you want to grow, how competitive your sector is and the capacity you have to deliver on new sales. Some FMCG or direct to consumer brands might need to allocate closer to 20% to break through in competitive markets.

If you're planning to allocate marketing budget as a percentage of revenue, I would suggest 8% as the sweet spot with it being spent on everything from research, brand development, design, campaigns and events.

But is there a better way to set a marketing budget?

Use customer lifetime value (CLTV) to guide your marketing budget planning. Customer lifetime value is the metric that shows you the likely total revenue one customer can bring into your business. It looks at the customer's likely revenue and their lifespan as a customer.

To calculate customer lifetime value you need to calculate average purchase value, and then multiply that number by the average purchase frequency to determine the overall customer value. Next you need to work out your average customer lifespan and finally multiply that by customer value. Then you'll have your average customer lifetime value.

Average purchase value: Divide your brand's total annual revenue by the number of purchases over that time.

Average purchase frequency rate: Divide the number of purchases by the number of unique customers who made those purchases.

Customer value: Multiply the average purchase value by the average purchase frequency rate.

Average customer lifespan: Work out the average number of years a customer stays with your company.

Calculate CLTV: The final step is to multiply customer value by the average customer lifespan.

Using CLTV you can invest properly into the customer relationship. Rather than focusing on ROI of one transaction you're taking into consideration the true value of building a relationship with a single customer. Often companies don't invest enough into acquiring customers through marketing because they look at the short term value of the customer acquisition. Customer Acquisition Cost (CAC) is a commonly measured metric in business and rightfully so but is usually based on ad spend, which is a short term view.

Perhaps the marketing budget question should be reframed to "how much can we afford to spend to acquire this valuable customer profitably?"

Defining ROI

"The business that can spend the most to acquire a customer wins." – Dan Kennedy.

This quote pops up in publications like Russell Brunson's book Dotcom Secrets and is a refreshing take on marketing. In a race to reduce customer acquisition costs, marketers are cutting corners to drive better campaign ROI.

The best way to increase ROI in marketing is usually to reduce spending. But if your competitors are spending more than you to acquire the same customer from the same audience you run the risk of losing out on an opportunity where had you spent a little more you could be serving them. It's time to rethink ROI as a longer term objective alongside shorter term metrics like clicks and cart abandonment. Serving your audience and acquiring new customers to join your tribe is a long term game, it's not just about click through rates and conversions.

Despite some questionable tax avoidance and working conditions, Amazon is a great example of spending more on acquiring customers. They famously refused to make a profit, instead reinvesting money into creating a better customer experience and offering. You too can become a dominant brand in your sector through profit reinvestment and knowing your acquisition cost limits.

Reinvest into marketing. Reinvest profits in your product, personal development, workforce training and new marketing strategies. Any way you can use your marketing budget to better serve your audience will be an investment in your brand that will be repaid.

The ROI of marketing should be based on how well you're serving your audience. Yes, there is a need to measure the return on investment of individual campaigns but marketers and entrepreneurs need to see the bigger picture beyond short term campaign metrics.

Optimise your marketing spending over time

Now you know how much you need to spend on marketing to be effective, the next step is to look at how to spend your budget more effectively. Continuous marketing improvement removes wastage in your marketing process. Your marketing spending is one place where waste can soon build up.

Using The Continuous Marketing Improvement Loop to manage marketing spending, you can remove wasteful spending on tactics and platforms that don't work. By measuring the effectiveness and iterating you're able to identify weak performing areas of your marketing plan and reinvest the money you save into more effective channels.

A 2015 Winterberry Group report found on average a marketer uses more than 12 different tools to manage campaigns and data, with some using more than 31. That's scary. Not all of them will be paid for tools but they will all have a time spend attached to them. Remove the tools and software you don't use much or switch to a cheaper alternative by looking at the product features you actually use. Reducing software spend is an easy way to free up money for more impactful marketing activity.

When you're using free tools like Mailchimp it's important to remember that you might need to upgrade to paid for packages in future as your brand grows. Consider such upgrade costs when you're looking at free options. If you've built your business on a platform it should scale with you and budgeting for these costs should be part of your marketing planning.

Test small with advertising. The great thing about social media advertising is you can experiment without spending huge amounts of money. Having said that, you should never promote or boost a post to increase your reach without a clear plan. The number of small businesses wasting money on Facebook boosts is scary. Click and hope is not a strategy you should be using in your business.

Another way to optimise marketing spending is by outsourcing marketing. Weighing up the costs of outsourcing and doing marketing in house is a consideration that should be thought through carefully. Depending on the size of your organisation and the amount of time and staff you have available to support marketing, you need to make a decision whether it is more cost effective and productive to outsource your marketing. Do you have the time and expertise to handle your marketing strategy from start to finish? Can you manage all of your channels properly to serve your audience effectively? If the answer is no, it might be time to consider working with a marketing agency.

CHAPTER 14
Use ethical marketing to become a no brainer

Amplifying your message to reach more people is vital to the survival of your brand and the delivery of the purpose you set out at the Define stage of this plan. Amplify isn't just about adopting endless tactics in pursuit of new customers, it's about using ethical marketing to drive real value in your interactions with your audience.

Amplify helps you acquire new customers and keep existing ones ethically.

Be the best in your industry at a small number of tactics

Don't spread yourself too thin.

Choose the right channels and focus on where you can add the most value. Unless you have a huge budget you can't win at everything. GymShark does events. Hubspot does content. Nike does advertising. Be good at a select few tactics.

Unless you have a big marketing team or you employ the services of a marketing agency you're going to struggle to effectively manage multiple tactics across your digital and offline channels.

Using the Continuous Marketing Improvement Loop, identify which tactics are working, which ones aren't and think carefully about whether you should drop a channel completely if it's not delivering on your marketing objectives or adding to your customer experience.

FOMO (Fear Of Missing Out) can get to us all as marketers and you're probably going to feel it when you're thinking about channels. You'll see someone on YouTube telling you they're smashing it on Tik Tok, you might see someone on LinkedIn say you need to be using paid social advertising. Think carefully before you add new tactics. Think about the audience you serve and whether it's a good fit for them. Do they hang out on these platforms? Do they want you to be adding value for them there? Or are they happy engaging with you where they are already? Just because someone else is doing something in your space, doesn't mean you should be doing it too.

Own the tactics you choose and push to be the best wherever you choose to invest your resources.

Planning your digital marketing campaigns

Every business needs marketing campaigns to acquire new customers and retain existing ones. Campaigns provide a vehicle to achieve your overall business strategy. By having a succinct online value proposition, you can reach more customers and grow your presence. Not having a set process for planning and executing your marketing campaigns is a very very bad idea. Why? You have no way to consistently approach your campaigns to make sure they deliver the same impact for your brand every single time you launch a new marketing programme.

Following a simple 7 step plan can be the difference between digital marketing campaign success and failure.

Step One - Objectives: You can't start a campaign without having a goal in mind for what you want to achieve. Follow a SMART strategy for creating your objectives. Making them Specific, Measurable, Achievable, Relevant and Time-focused.   With objectives, you can be as ambitious or as practical as you like, but knowing what you want to achieve will help you to prepare your budget and gives your digital marketing campaign a journey to follow to get there.

Step Two - Know Your Processes: Without knowing your sales funnel and customer interaction points, you will not be able to target and nurture leads with the right content at the right time. Taking time to examine the process, the interactions and the journey for leads can help you to work out where your digital marketing will be most effective and what individual stages need focus.

Working out where your content is most effective and where it isn't hitting the mark is useful, not just for this campaign but for campaigns in the future too.

Step Three - Collate Resources: Make your campaign much easier and cheaper by utilising the information you already have. Branding guides, previous digital marketing content, brochures and documents can all serve to help your digital marketing campaign. Once collated, work out how they can benefit your campaign to ensure that you extract all the possible value out of your current information to save money and make your campaign run smoother.

Step Four - Reinforce Your USP: When setting up your business, it is likely that you identified your unique selling point. As the business progresses and work gets in the way, you may have lost sight of what makes your business different. However, in order to make a digital marketing campaign a success, you need to reinforce your USP and why your customers should buy from you. Make sure you're clear on your proposition so that it can shine throughout your campaign and all of your digital marketing content.

Step Five - Measure Your Success: Measuring your success through key performance indicators is vital for you to determine what is working well in your campaign and what you need to improve. Without measures you won't know where to focus your budget or attention, resulting in wasted time, money and effort and a poorly performing marketing strategy.

With KPIs in place, you can tailor and tweak your campaign as you go, ensuring that you maximise your investment.

Step Six - Content Calendar: A major aspect of your digital marketing campaign will be your content. Content isn't a one-off job in your campaign, it will require constant commitment. A key aspect of your campaign will be to produce content on an ongoing basis. To keep your content on track and to ensure it remains sustainable, use a content calendar. This will allow you to outsource, budget and allocate time better.

Remember, as your audience grows, content requirements will too. So it may be helpful to come up with a complete content strategy to make sure you can always commit to your content and don't leave it to fall behind.

Step Seven - Understand Your Buyers: Not all of your buyers, leads and audience will fall under the same category. There will be groups and segments within your audience, and you'll want to make sure that they are all catered for. Creating buyer personas (discussed earlier in this book) for these groups and segments can be invaluable in determining which digital marketing approaches to follow and tactics to include. You can then develop specific strategies to suit each buyer persona.

Glastonbury, Parklife & Creamfields

What do all of these brands have in common?

They use tension to sell. In his book Oversubscribed, Daniel Priestley talks about the way festivals and events use tension to sell tickets. They use staged releases to sell hundreds of thousands of tickets within minutes.

How? They define capacity, build tension then release. In your business you will have a limited capacity to deliver true value. The first stage of using tension in your marketing is to define your capacity. How many paying customers can you serve? How many people can you service to your best standards?

Once you've defined your capacity, let the world know you have limited space on your next client intake, product launch or programme. We covered the concept of supply and demand in economics earlier in this book. This concept reverses the effect of competitive markets. By reducing capacity, you're able to charge a price based on value rather than a market driven price.

Use a timeline of releases, events and communications to sell out your product or service when release date comes.

I'm not a fan of Elon Musk but I can appreciate that he's a great marketer and visionary. Maybe the pot helps? Who knows. But what I do know is that he has used tension to build a brand, and has developed Tesla into a cult with die hard fans that live and breathe the Tesla brand.

How? Using pre release and limited capacity in the same way that festivals do. He uses events, pre launch and pre ordering to show the rest of the market that others want his product. This sends a signal to others in the car market, making them believe that "if other people want this car I want it to."

You pull a slingshot as far back as possible until it's ready to snap, then you release it to go further. The same principle applies in marketing. Create tension to go further. It's a simple but effective concept.

Build tension then release. Don't release until you've overfilled your capacity. Wait until you have more buyers than product or service availability and you'll always have a buzz around your brand. Tension is a simple but powerful concept that works for festivals and brands alike.

Events

Events can add huge value to your audience, they give you the chance to entertain, educate and inspire a room full of people. A room full of your ideal customers. A room full of people who care about what you're doing.

Thought leadership events are a great way to serve your audience while building your brand and authority within your niche. They also offer a chance for your attendees to expand their knowledge, creating a more empowered audience.

In 2019, Elon launched the Tesla CyberTruck to the world with 250,000 pre orders. Now he tweeted this so they're not official figures but even if Tesla got half of those pre orders the launch was a success. How do you pre sell 250,000 vehicles before even building them? Combining the power of events and tension. What people want is what other people want. He used the "screen break" to generate media attention and a polarising product to generate sales. Referencing Elon Musk in two sections of this chapter. Lucky guy.

It doesn't matter if you're a B2B or a B2C brand, you can run experiential events to engage your audience.

Gymshark has turned online retail on its head with their use of events and influencers. Thousands of fans flock to their events in the hope of seeing their favourite influencers or buying a unique tee printed in the same way Ben Francis printed his first products. They use events as a way to get closer to their audience. According to the company, these events are loss making yet they continue to run them in cities across the globe. Why? Because they're an extremely valuable way to build relationships and humanise the brand.

Evoke a reaction to promote an action

People have decision fatigue, we scroll past social posts and click away from blogs within seconds if they don't resonate. Marketers need to make their audience feel something to make a change in their habits. Break the cycle of endless scrolling by making your target pause.

Conversion rate optimisation (CRO) is an effective way to boost interaction and conversion on your website. CRO tests colours, messaging and calls to action to produce better results. This thinking should be applied to all of your marketing. You can optimise almost every marketing tool to be more effective.

Calls to action across your website and other channels need to evoke an emotional reaction to promote an action. Call to action buttons should sell a positive outcome and messaging should be positive to build trust in your solution.

Use social proof

First seen in the book Influence written in 1984 by Robert Cialdini, social proof refers to the way in which people copy the actions of others. According to Robert, we see an action as being more correct if we see someone else performing it too.

Social proof helps build trust with your audience. There are numerous ways you can use it in your brand. Expert social proof is when an expert or thought leader in your industry recommends your brand or leaves a review endorsing your products or services. Influencer social proof is another form of social proof. When influencers are associated with your brand they lend their audience's trust to you. Being open and honest about paid influencer partnerships is essential for social proof to work effectively.

Your audience is also one of the biggest sources of social proof. User social proof is when your customer recommends your brand or leaves a review online. This is probably the best form of social proof you can get. Your audience is powerful, a vote of confidence from them speaks volumes.

Big followings on social media have been counted as social proof in the past but a following means nothing without great engagement. Those who have bought followers are seeing their authority falling on social networks. Social proof comes from genuine endorsements of your brand. But brands are using social proof irresponsibly. Overinflating "X people are viewing this page" and "X just bought this product" are just a couple of ways brands are using social proof unethically online.

If we don't use social proof responsibly and ethically as marketers its effect will be diminished and it will be another tactic buyers don't trust.

Backup your message with evidence

If you're in B2B use case study videos and project highlights. B2B marketing is all about building relationships and nurturing contacts until they're ready to buy. Producing case study content builds trust and proves to a prospect you're the ideal brand to work with.

Often, in B2B buying situations there are multiple decision makers. Producing helpful visual and written content enables the person driving the buying process forward to win the buy in of other stakeholders and decision makers in the business.

If you're in B2C or technology use real customer reviews to show how others within your audience use your brand to solve their problems. Instead of writing about your product benefits, show people how your product benefits others. Using customer reviews on product pages can increase conversion and reduce bounce rates.

Ethical marketing is guided by 20 principles

Treat your audience with respect: The first rule is to always have your audience in mind whenever you embark on a new marketing campaign or start planning new products or services. When you're thinking about the effects of your decisions on your audience you're being respectful. Always be honest and open with them and treat them with the respect you expect from the brands you buy from.

Be honest: Being honest is the easiest way to win the trust of your audience. Sometimes things go wrong or you might not be quite where you want to be in terms of sustainability.

The best brands are honest and tell their customers the truth. If they messed up an order, they own up to it and rectify the issue. If they can't find a suitable sustainable packaging option at the moment, they will tell you that they're working on it. Be honest.

Be transparent: Transparency is similar to honesty. Share what's going on behind the scenes in your brand. Open up your process to your audience and be transparent with progress you're making to deliver a better customer experience.

Use storytelling in your marketing campaigns to build a deeper more transparent connection with your audience.

Don't oversell and underdeliver: The first rule of marketing? Don't oversell and underdeliver. Believe it or not some brands still do this, they promise the customer the earth and deliver an experience below the customer's expectations. Disappointing customers is unethical and should have no place in a modern marketing driven brand.

Use your marketing to sell the benefits of your product, don't over promise in your marketing copy. Be honest and focus on facts. There's enough fake news around we don't need unethical marketing messages adding to it.

Don't sell sh*t stuff: Similar to the last point, don't sell rubbish products or services. There are enough subpar products in the world already, your customers don't need more of them. To be an ethical marketer you need to produce great products and services that meet and exceed the expectations of your customers.

Own up when you make mistakes: Things go wrong in business. We've all received a late delivery or a broken product in the post. Own the mistake (even if it's your courier's fault) and rectify the issue for your customer. If you have a customer service team, give them the authority to help the customer and give them the tools they need to deliver a great customer experience.

Value time and attention: As a marketer you have the unique power to take away someone's time. The ads, the website copy and the emails you send take away your audience's time and attention. Value that time by adding real value to their day. Make sure your ads are truthful and reach the right people. Make sure your ad landing pages match up to your ads so you've not wasted someone's time when they click through to find you aren't going to deliver the value you offered in your advertisement copy.

Be authentic: Don't be something you're not as a brand. Brands need to reinvent themselves to stay alive in fast paced industries but that doesn't mean you shouldn't be authentic to yourself. If you've been using a specific tone of voice for the last few years, don't suddenly change it to become hip and trendy. Be true to yourself while innovating to deliver a better customer experience

Go beyond profit: Marketing is about delivering change. Change in a buyer's state. Change in someone's wealth, opportunities or needs. When you focus on delivering change marketing takes on a whole new meaning.

Go beyond marketing objectives and focus on how you can add real value with your marketing. The best ethical marketers don't focus solely on profit, they focus on how they can go beyond profit to deliver real change.

Care about the impact you have on others: Marketing affects everyone. From the people seeing your ads on social platforms and the customers who buy your products to the environmental impact of your marketing decisions. Ethical marketing is about considering and caring about the impact you have on others and the environment. Plan and execute your marketing in a way that takes into consideration those that you might affect.

Be nice: To succeed in marketing you need to win the buy in from other functions within your business. You need to inspire others to commit to the same ethical practice you live by. Being nice is an easy way to build relationships with others who have an impact on the way you market and deliver an ethical customer experience.

Stick to your values: Value driven marketing is the easiest way to market ethically. By focusing on your own values and those of your organisation you can use these values as a guiding light for any marketing decisions you make. If an action doesn't align with the values you've set, don't do it.

Educate others: As a great marketer, you have a duty to educate others. If you've learnt something valuable, share it with others so they can get value from it too. Content marketing is a great way to educate others, use your brand's website to share the unique knowledge you have in your industry. Pass on the best tips and advice to really add value to your audience.

Inspire action: By using ethical marketing and storytelling you're able to inspire others to take action on the things that matter to you as a marketer. You can inspire people to do more for the planet, to be more compassionate or to tell their friends about your product or service.

Be proud of your place in the world: Using ethical marketing means you're behaving in a way you can be proud of. You're rising above the underhand tactics used by others and you're delivering value to your audience by marketing ethically. Be proud of the work you're doing and do more of it.

Don't use underhand tactics: Don't resort to using underhand tactics used by unethical marketers. Don't rely on constant sales promotions to win new customers. Don't use false advertising to sell benefits your product or service doesn't deliver. Don't use false scarcity on your product pages, if you have 12,727 products left, don't say only 5 left. If you haven't got any reviews yet, don't make them up.

Use your common sense when it comes to choosing which marketing practices are ethical and which aren't.

Stay with your goals: It's tempting to flit to the latest trends and new marketing tool but to win the attention of your target audience and convert them to customers you need to do your time. You need to invest your energy into building trust and strong relationships. Don't flit to the latest shiny object like other marketers, focus on your goals and work relentlessly to achieve them by serving your audience.

Don't be influenced by bad marketers: It's easy to see other marketers in your industry doing well in your industry and cut corners on your ethics. Focus on your values and the reasons why you don't want to market unethically. Bad marketers might make short term wins but great businesses thrive on building long lasting relationships with their customers, something you're doing by using ethical marketing.

Use data ethically: GDPR should have put an end to unethical use of data but it hasn't. Companies are still misusing data and contacting customers who haven't opted in to receive marketing communication. Use data ethically and treat it with care. Use a CRM system to keep customer data safe and only contact customers who have given you prior permission to communicate with them.

Serve your audience: Finally, to win at marketing today you need to focus on how you can serve your audience. Great marketers serve their audience instead of looking internally. To reach marketing objectives you need to first look at the objectives of your target audience, what do they need to thrive? What do they want and desire? Your job as an ethical marketer is to serve your audience and deliver on their needs and wants over a long period of time to win attention, trust and loyalty.

A new kind of top of mind

Top of mind awareness (TOMA) refers to a brand or specific product being first in a customer's mind when thinking of a particular industry or category.

Being the no brainer and automatic thought in your sector is the ultimate goal in marketing. It's the dream of brands across the world. Think trainers, think Nike. Think gym, think Pure Gym. Think electric car, think Tesla. Top of mind brands get the best opportunities and grow quicker than their competition.

How? Traditional brands would use advertising or following customers around constantly to reach top of mind status. But there's an ethical alternative, be the mate your audience goes to for advice, the one who always has their back.

When brands use advertising they're usually starting the buying journey off for competitors. Those who have a better marketing strategy will usually pick up the customer, even though the advertisement was what prompted the buyer's action. This is why building relationships with your audience and embedding yourself is so important, the content you put out over time, the social media posts you create and the emails you send to your email list all help to build you as the no brainer in your sector.

Delivering value over time is the simplest way to achieve top of mind status. You've helped your audience and when the time is right, they will reward you by thinking of you first when they have a problem that needs fixing.

Ungating content

A lead magnet is an offer of value in exchange for a person's contact information, it could be in the form of a PDF, swipe file of templates or video content.

Lead magnets have become mainstream in marketing over the years with Ryan Diess of Digital Marketer fame pushing more and more brands to use them to generate more leads and interest in their business. While they can add immense value to your audience when well written and produced properly, the power of the lead magnet is diminishing.

Information is becoming less valuable and people can now access a lot of the information contained in lead magnets free on the internet. Serve your audience by ungating your content. Remove the barrier to download it and give it to your audience in your blog posts, videos or social posts without the need for contact information.

Some people thought Volvo had gone mad when it gave away its invention - the three point seatbelt. Instead it built their reputation as a caring, safe car brand and helped them sell millions of cars. If they can give away a multi million dollar idea, I'm sure you can give away some of your content for the benefit of your business and your audience.

Choosing tactics

Your industry, budget and audience will dictate what tactics work and don't work for your brand. When you're choosing tactics, you need to have two questions in mind. Who is my audience and where are they?

Choosing tactics will of course be guided by your strategy but the easiest way to reach customers is to find where they're hanging out already. Don't look to interrupt them. Look at how you can add value with your marketing.

Every business is different but there are a few tactics that are effective in specific industries.

E-commerce: Social media marketing works particularly well alongside influencer marketing to show how people use a brand's products. Equally, Google Shopping campaigns and content marketing can be effective.

B2B: Social media marketing and LinkedIn in particular are great ways to market a business to business brand. Turn employees and brand leaders into thought leaders by posting regular helpful content to your network. LinkedIn allows you to build personal connections with decision makers and like minded people.

Build partnerships

The chances are you're not alone in seeking the change you want to make in the world, find other brands who care about the same things and work together. You can become an unstoppable force when you work together. Partnerships are a powerful marketing tool. How can you work together to better serve both of your audiences?

Work with upstream services or others with similar interests. Upstream services are brands who sell into your audience further up the chain to you. For example, in B2B a web design company might partner with a hosting company or domain registration company to pass leads between each other. They might co brand marketing campaigns to share the marketing costs and knowledge learnt from the campaign.

Influencers are another example of partnerships that can drive your marketing. Build transparent relationships with authorities in your sector and those who your audience respect. Move away from a transactional relationship with influencers, instead focus on building relationships with a select number of influencers who can become real brand ambassadors. The best brands work across multiple campaigns over time rather than one off paid for endorsements.

Brand loyalty is the new key to success

What do Casper and Warby Parker have in common? Firstly they're both direct to consumer brands. Secondly, they have used purpose and a better shopping experience to build a seriously big base of brand ambassadors.

They saw that their audience wasn't interested in product features alone and built an emotional connection with them by creating an engaging customer experience from the product, ordering, delivery and marketing processes. Customer focused companies are putting brand engagement ahead of sales focused relationships and they're seeing the benefits with brand loyalty and love.

In order to do the same you need to ask yourself, "do my audience understand who we are and what we're about? Are they excited about us existing and why? How can we use marketing to build a connection beyond a transactional relationship?"

Stop pronouncing tactics dead

I saw someone say content marketing was dead and decided it should now be called Knowledge Marketing. Cool name but why? Content marketing isn't dead. Just like print marketing isn't. In a bid to stamp their mark on ideas they pronounce the existing tactic or tool dead. Be known as a marketer that markets ethically, instead of thinking you're better than other marketers who use traditional tactics by pronouncing the death of the tactics they use.

Find tactics that work for you and your brand and let others do their thing too. Nothing has to die for you to be effective at marketing.

The big SEO myth

If people are in the market for your product or service, they're actively searching for a way to solve their problem. Google offers you the perfect opportunity to get in front of them and sell. Or so you might think. Brands spend millions of pounds every year trying to get to the first page of Google, some do it well and others don't. Competition for the top spots on page one is fierce and even once you've got there it doesn't guarantee success, the visitor comes to your site, has a look around and disappears never to be seen again.

Search engine optimisation (SEO) needs to be part of a clear digital marketing strategy. You need to have a great website that converts, helpful content to build trust and a strong message to stand a chance of winning a customer straight from a Google search. Tactics like retargeting can help you get back lost visitors but even then the buyer might not be ready to buy. Your strategy should incorporate nurturing with social media and email marketing too. As you can see, even when you get to the top of the rankings, it's not as easy as sitting back and watching the leads batter down your door.

You need to be top of mind in your industry. SEO is a part of that but without brand recognition and trust among your audience you're not going to convert organic search traffic to paying customers. This is why defining the audience you want to serve is so important. If you're trying to target everyone, you're going to struggle to stay top of mind for them. By owning your space and being specific about what you do and who you do it for, you stand a much better chance of being the brand of choice when your ideal customer does decide they want to solve a problem.

Using social media properly

Too many brands use social as a sales platform, as a megaphone to shout about the organisation's latest offers and deals to their audience. Instead of using social media to push out tired sales messages, build genuine connections with your audience and provide real value before you even think about asking for a sale. Answer questions, create polls, inspire them with stories and educate them with tips to make their lives easier. The word social should really give you a clue as to what it should be used for. Be sociable. Don't be that guy who comes to the party to sell his latest pyramid scheme.

It's easy for smaller brands and startups to see established brands using social media as a sales channel but they've established themselves in their sector already and have earned the trust of their audience. New entrants don't have that luxury, so invest your time in building an engaged following on social media before you jump into product or service promotional marketing.

CHAPTER 15
Become a storyteller

Stories are vital to the success of brands.

Storytelling helps you build a connection with potential customers and stand out in increasingly competitive markets. From fashion ecommerce stores to B2B brands, storytelling is becoming more common.

It's time for you to start telling your unique brand story.

The problem with websites

Most websites aren't using storytelling and it's resulting in high bounce rates, poor conversion rates and a bad customer experience.

We've all been to sites after clicking on a social ad. We click around, look at a few pages but soon get bored and click back to what we were doing.

Why?

While there are lots of reasons people don't use the buy or contact function on websites, one of the biggest challenges for website owners is grabbing someone's attention and keeping it. Most sites are set up to focus on the brand's products or services, not what makes the brand unique.

The importance of storytelling

If you've ever watched an episode of the X Factor you'll know all about the story. Humans are fine tuned to absorb stories much more easily than facts and statistics. Stories make us sit up and pay attention, we connect with them on some level and we retain them in our minds.

If a story is framed correctly and told in the right way, a brand can connect with a consumer and build a two way conversation. This is something that is vital in order to stand out and build customer loyalty over time. Think John Lewis adverts, they're not heavily product focused but we remember them and share them with our loved ones. Why? Because as well as hearing, reading and seeing stories we all love telling them too.

Your consumers become your brand ambassadors by sharing the story of your brand to their friends, family and work colleagues. That's how messages spread, through the power of storytelling. Your brand can utilise this powerful tool too.

Why do brands use stories?

If you've ever read any fictional story you'll know how intensely you can feel the experience you're reading about, as if it is actually happening to you.

When the brain detects an emotionally charged event, the amygdala releases dopamine into the system. Because dopamine greatly aids memory and information processing, you could say it creates a Post It note that reads, 'Remember this.'"

John Medina, Brain Rules

Brands use stories to tune us into their message, to feel some sort of connection with them through the shared experience of a story.

The beginning, middle & end

To connect with customers you need to be the brand to solve a specific problem they have. So you need to create a story with a beginning, middle and end (the problem, your solution and the results).

Beginning: The Problem: identify who your customers are, what specific pain points they have and why they care enough to make a change in their lives.

Middle: Your Solution & Promise: craft your message around your customer, what is your reason for wanting to help them? Why are you the best person to help them? Are your reasons personal? What are you promising you will do to help your customer solve their problem?

End: Your Customers' Results: this is where your story spreads. By being remarkable and delivering on the promise you made to help your customer solve a problem you're creating a way for your idea to spread to more and more people.

Communicating your story

To connect with your audience you're going to need to use some storytelling tactics used by successful brands.

Craft a unique personality: brands who are smashing their marketing have personality. Think Gymshark, Aldi, Spotify and Paddy Power - they all know who they are and use imagery and content to share their message consistently. They stay true to their brand and communicate authentically.

Be value driven: by focusing on values that resonate with your customer you can make value based decisions when you're communicating. Does this fit with what my customers value? No. Don't do it.

Make it easy for your customers to share your story: the easiest way to spread stories is by having other people share them for you. Make it easy for your customers to spread the word by going above and beyond your brand promises.

Your customers are your story.

Your story isn't set in stone, it should evolve over time. Stick to your core values but innovate and respond to changes. Brands who will survive in times of uncertainty are those who have a deep connection with their customers and ones who adapt to their ever changing needs.

Stories increase trust & authenticity

By creating an authentic story you help build trust with your audience and they feel connected to your brand. Authenticity is key here. If you create a fictional story and your audience sees through it, you'll automatically lose trust. Once trust is lost it's hard to rebuild. Make sure your story is authentic and easy to tell to build trust across your audience.

Stories increase brand loyalty

Brands who build relationships with their customers have greater brand loyalty. Brands like Apple and Patagonia have built a following of dedicated fans. Apple fans still camp out overnight for the latest iPhone, Macbook or iPad and Patagonia has dedicated followers who want to save the planet. Both brands use storytelling as a way to grow brand loyalty beyond products.

Stories help buyers take action

With so much choice and information available to consumers they often put off buying decisions because of the stress involved in making a decision. By creating a compelling story you make the decision to choose your brand much easier by cutting through the marketing noise and appealing to the head and the heart of consumers.

Start with "Why"

The unique passions, interests and experiences behind your business will shape its reason for existing. Every business has a reason to exist, else there's not much point in it being there.

What drove you to set up your business?

What does your business care about?

What values do you and your business follow?

Once you've answered the questions above you should have the basics of a "Why." You'll probably need to refine this further to get a compelling answer to the question "Why does my business exist?"

Let your customers' needs shape your story

There is nothing more valuable to your business than your customers and their stories. Ask for reviews, ask them why they use your products and find out what makes them choose you. Build your story around your customers' stories.

Do they buy your organic t shirts because it makes them feel like they're contributing to moving the fashion industry away from fast fashion? Do they buy your food because it reminds them of a special time in their lives? Listen to your customers and use their reasons for using your products and services in your storytelling.

You'll notice patterns in the reasons why customers buy from you - use these to create a story that resonates and connects with your customers.

Be part of something bigger

Storytelling doesn't always have to focus on your specific company, it can be a part of something bigger. For example, the war on plastics is a huge subject and has huge players like David Attenborough engaging to tackle the problem. Your brand can join in that conversation to become part of the story.

How can your organisation contribute to reducing plastics, or how can your brand partner with others to be part of something bigger?

Focus on emotions

For stories to connect with consumers you need to focus on what emotion you want them to feel. What do you want your customers to feel when they use your product? Build that into your product or service to bring about an emotion when someone engages with your brand. Always focus on positive emotions, we don't want someone to feel sad or angry when they use our product. We want them to feel something positive.

Make it shareable

All good stories are concise and memorable which makes them easy to share. Your consumers become your biggest brand ambassadors, reducing your marketing costs and increasing awareness of your story and brand.

When someone feels good about using your product they're much more likely to share their experience with their network. You could try using a branded hashtag to get consumers sharing their positive experiences on social media. Brand hashtags are great for platforms like Instagram and Pinterest.

Storytelling in practice

Patagonia

Patagonia is often used as an example of a brand doing great things for the environment. Their storytelling and transparency has led them to become a brand loved by millions. So how do they do it?

Everything Patagonia does builds its brand story as a premium sustainable and ethical apparel company. From their use of materials to environmental policies and supply chain transparency they have cornered the environmentally-conscious apparel market and they continue to grow while being ethical.

While their products speak for themselves in terms of quality and how long they last, the real value in the brand is through its storytelling. Everyone says they want to save the planet but everything Patagonia does suggests that they really do. They have invested millions of pounds into sustainable startups and have even given away IP rights to other companies when it can benefit the environment and help others (sometimes competitors) to innovate and produce more environmentally friendly products.

Their use of video and aspirational imagery is key to their storytelling success. They regularly commission videos to promote their campaigns and impact on the environment. As demographics and values change, more and more people are buying into Patagonia's story and that story is spreading like wildfire, resulting in more sales and bigger profits.

Doing good in business really does deliver.

Warby Parker

Who'd have thought you could build a story around glasses?

Well two students in America did and they had a simple story "Glasses are too expensive". Tied in with a Buy 1, Give 1 model - they had a strong story that resonated.

From inception the brand focused on creating a more affordable way to buy glasses and people stood up and listened. Through the use of social media storytelling they built a brand following of over 500k followers on Instagram.

Their use of boomerangs and stories on Instagram is one way they use ecommerce storytelling to engage their audience. Warby Parker uses video differently across platforms, opting for shorter snappy storytelling clips on Instagram and more shareable long form video on Facebook.

What do these brands have in common?

They communicate a consistent story across different channels by tailoring the way the message is delivered on each platform. They focus on the consumer and what they care about to deliver a story that resonates using personal and impactful copywriting.

If you're ready to grow your brand, you should consider adding storytelling to your marketing strategy. The power of stories to build relationships and spread awareness is huge.

CHAPTER 16
The world needs more content creators

Content is all around us.

From blogs to videos to social media posts we consume different forms of content everyday. Those memes you liked on Facebook are content, the latest make up tutorial you just followed is content and the podcast you listen to religiously is content.

The best marketers are content creators who serve their audience.

They give back to their audience with content, they produce, write and put together content for others to consume, like and share.

To succeed in marketing you need to be like them. Become a content creator.

What is content creation?

Content creation is the process of creating content in a format your audience can consume. It could be in the form of a blog, video, podcast or infographic or any one of lots of other formats.

Not only is it an effective way to engage with potential customers and demonstrate your expertise in your area, it also gives you a chance to provide real value.

- What knowledge could you pass onto your audience?

- What information is your audience crying out for?

- What content would your audience really find valuable?

Your audience is waiting for you to serve them, to answer their questions and provide them with information that entertains, educates or inspires them.

The world needs more content creators

Why? For a few reasons.

Most content marketing is rubbish

We're bombarded with and overwhelmed by the number of marketing messages we see every day. The answer? Producing content that isn't directly selling or marketing to a potential customer. While in practice this sounds good, the truth is most content marketing is rubbish and marketers are still using it to promote their products and services.

The power of content marketing is in the trust it builds with your audience. The connection you can build with readers, viewers and listeners of your content is invaluable. Without providing value with your content you're missing out on a huge opportunity to build those relationships and connections.

According to Demand Metric in 2013 90% of all organisations use content in their marketing efforts. But that doesn't mean 90% of organisations using content marketing are good at it. Far from it. New blogs are produced everyday. New memes. New YouTube content. How many of those go unnoticed? How many of those are ignored by their target audience?

Brands and people currently succeeding in content creation are those who really understand their audience and produce content they love. Not those that use their influence to push sales messages or produce poorly planned and executed content.

You have a story that needs to be told

Every person and brand has a unique story to be told. You have a unique set of people who you can reach with that story. It's your duty to tell your story.

Because it's good for business

I'm not suggesting you get started with content creation for the sake of it. There needs to be good reason to invest time, money and effort into content marketing and the main reason... it's good for business.

According to US agency Demand Metric, Content marketing generates 3x as many leads as traditional marketing with businesses who use it winning 126% more leads that ones that don't. Oh and it costs 62% less than traditional marketing tactics like TV and digital advertising.

Strategy before creation

Before getting stuck into creating content, it's important to follow a proven content marketing process to make sure your content resonates and answers your audience's needs.

As I've mentioned a few times in this book, the starting point of any successful marketing campaign is strategy. No jumping straight into writing or posting to social media. A successful brand strategy includes everything from your marketing objectives to how you will promote your content.

Setting clear objectives beyond serving your audience

Start with asking the question - why am I using content marketing?

This will help you generate a starting point to form your content objectives. Just like any other marketing objective, your content marketing objectives need to be SMART goals. You could aim to increase social media following by 30% by the end of November. Or you could set an objective to grow organic traffic by 20% with content in the next 3 months.

Once you've set your objectives you have a purpose and reason for all of the content you are going to produce, beyond the obvious goal of contributing to your audience.

Identify who wants your content

Everything we do in marketing should be about serving our audience and to do that we need to know who they are.

Every effective marketing campaign is based on one thing. Speaking directly to your target customer. And to do that, you need to really understand who your audience are and why they care about what you have to say.

Using the buyer personas you have already created, you will have a clear image of the person you want to focus your content creation efforts around. So how do you gather important persona details without spending hours conducting customer interviews?

Surveys

Surveys are invaluable to business. Free software like SurveyMonkey has made it easier than ever to ask questions and gather information. You can put together a set of questions to help build a picture of your audience.

You might include questions on their demographic including age and location. As well as some specific product/service based questions specific to your industry. Why do they use certain products at the moment? What are there strongest beliefs?

Your questions should allow you to build a profile of your ideal customers based on common themes in respondents' answers.

Industry publications/sites

Most industries already have an established source of trusted information. Whether it's a news site or blog, you can rely on these sources to give you up to date information on what is happening in your industry.

Use these sites by looking at their most popular articles, read the comments to see what people have to say. You'll be surprised how much people are willing to share about their problems and talk about themselves online.

Follow these sites on social media to see who is engaging and commenting. This allows you to build a good picture of the people who are interested in certain topics. You can then use them as a basis for a buyer persona.

Remember your buyers' stage in their buying journey

Buying journeys are becoming increasingly unpredictable.

The days of a buyer moving smoothly through a buying funnel are limited and instead marketers now face the challenge of trying to produce content to meet buyers at every stage in their buying journey.

Whilst it's impossible to produce content for every stage of the journey we know we can still split journeys into 3 loose categories. Awareness, Consideration and Decision.

Within these three groups, there are lots of factors that will affect the way someone will move through the journey. The bigger the pain, you'd expect the quicker someone would want to move towards a purchase. However, sometimes the biggest challenges and pains are the most important decisions. This means we need more information and detail before we can make such a decision.

Remembering the stage at which your buyer is at will guide your content marketing. Making sure you create content for each stage of the journey means they have all the information they need at every stage.

The buying journey also has an effect on the format of your content. At the awareness stage you might produce an infographic or blog post to help them understand their problem. Someone who has already identified they have a problem doesn't want you to list their problems, they want you to show them why you're the right person or company to solve them. At this stage you might use a PDF product guide to show the benefits of working with you.

Producing content

You've written a buyer persona and you've identified the different stages of your buyer's journey. It's time to get started producing content.

Keyword research

Your buyer persona research should have given you some idea of the issues your target customer cares about. While it would be nice if you just needed one customer to sustain your business, it's likely you're going to need a group of similar people to consume your content.

This is where keyword research comes in. This will tell you if a piece of content is worth writing about. Start by writing down some questions that your buyer persona might ask Google to help them solve their problem or to achieve their goals. Now you can use a piece of software like Moz Keyword Explorer to find the monthly search volume and keyword difficulty of keywords related to those questions.

Lots of SEO experts will tell you that keywords with less than 250 monthly searches aren't worth writing about. While everyone would love to have their content ranking for these searches, if you're just starting out the chances of you gaining a high volume, high competition keyword are low. That's why I suggest you focus on keywords with more than 50 monthly searches. There is search volume and you're much more likely to get your content ranking on Google and generating organic traffic to reach the objectives you set earlier to get your site ranked.

Generate ideas that connect

This is the fun part. Generating ideas that could become content.

The best starting point for this stage is going old school with a piece of paper and a mindmap. Group content in topic groups. For example, sustainability might be one topic cluster. From there you can break down groups to subtopics and more niche categories within the bigger group.

If you're struggling for ideas, a quick Google search of your chosen topic will give you content ideas from YouTube videos, news, blogs and guides. Don't copy them. Use them as inspiration for a starting point. Remember your content needs to be tailored to your buyer persona, so if you just copy someone else's content idea you're not producing content specifically for your target customer. Once you've got lots of ideas down on paper try to narrow them down to the best five. Decide on a title and what format the content should take. You can then move onto producing the piece of content.

Producing content

You've got a title and a format for your piece of content. It's now time to produce it.

I can't emphasise enough that you need to have your persona in mind at all times. Use language throughout that will connect with them. If you're using imagery, make sure you use photos and graphics that make sense and build a connection with your target audience. Most importantly, remember to serve your audience. You're not selling with this piece of content. You're trying to add value and help them. You're creating a unique, memorable piece of content that your audience is going to love.

Edit, edit, edit

Even the best writers and content creators in the world don't get it right first time.

The best pieces of content are those that are revisited and tweaked to make sure they hit the brief and meet the needs of your audience. The usual things need to be checked like grammar and spelling but you should also pay attention to the length of sentences, using enough whitespace and your tone of voice to make sure your content is easy to consume, understand and connect with.

Serving your content

You're ready to post your content, and whether you're uploading a blog post to your website or a video to YouTube you should have a consistent process.

If you're just starting out, this won't matter so much but when you're a more established content creator you should be doing research on the best time to post out content. For example on social media the best time to post your content is when most of your followers are online. Putting together a content calendar would be beneficial to make sure you're posting our your content consistently and regularly.

Promoting your content piece

You've researched buyer personas and you've produced a unique piece of content. Great. But without promoting it, chances are nobody is going to see your hard work.

Blog posts are great because they're picked up by search engines with little effort, your work is indexed and if you've written it well with good keyword research you stand a chance of it being ranked. But this takes time and it will take time to establish yourself as a go to in your industry.

So how else can you promote your content?

Start with your buyer persona. Where do your audience hang out? Do they use Facebook or Instagram? Do they use email or messenger? What time of day do they log on to check their social media?

All of these questions will help you identify the best place to promote your content.

Social Media

Social media is great for building connections with your audience. Most businesses still tend to use it to push out boring marketing messages instead of taking the opportunity to really add value to their audience.

Tailor your message across different platforms. If you're promoting ideas from your content on Instagram focus on imagery and short snappy takeaways. If you're using Facebook, use longer form content or memes to get the attention of your prospects.

Email

Email marketing has been pronounced dead several times but still seems to be around. Weird.

Email is one of the best ways to engage with your audience by building a community of like minded people who have opted to join your mailing list. Segment your list based on interests and send them links to content that you think your subscribers will love. Don't send mass emails or spam your list with promotional messages 24/7. Focus on creating a targeted, engaged group of people who love the content you produce.

Measuring content marketing impact

You've set objectives for your content marketing. This final stage of the content creation process is all about measuring those objectives and how well your content is performing to help you reach your goals.

The best thing about being a marketer today is the amount of data you have available to you. Tools like Google Analytics and Search Console allow you to drill down into how effectively your marketing is performing. You can measure everything from the amount of traffic generated from organic search, the number of email signups from a content piece, the bounce rate of people leaving your content without visiting another page to the number of shares a piece of content received.

All of this information is invaluable and starts to paint a picture of what does and doesn't resonate with your audience. If a piece of content you created has generated little traffic and has a high bounce rate it might mean people don't care about what you've written about. If your video has a low engagement rate it might be time to switch up your style or think up some new topics.

The power of iteration

All of your marketing information gives you the power to tweak your content until it's right. Too many business owners and marketers focus on producing the perfect image, video or blog. The truth is, most marketing is guesswork. Until you've produced something you don't 100% know if your audience will like it.

The good news though, is that by using data you can get better at knowing what your audience connects with and produce more content that does just this. By iterating and tweaking you can perfect your content creation process to build an unstoppable content marketing machine that adds value and smashes your marketing objectives.

Pull with inbound marketing

Inbound marketing has been lauded as the saviour of marketing for a good few years now but still most businesses are doing it badly. They do a bit of inbound marketing here and there and then revert to old sales tactics when results aren't instant.

When done correctly inbound marketing can give you a competitive advantage in your market and set you aside in your audience's mind. By harnessing the powers of tried-and-tested inbound marketing strategies, you can encourage customers to get in touch with you first. These strategies can be anything from blog writing and social media, to getting your branding right.

What is inbound marketing?

'[Inbound Marketing are] things you can do on the web that earn traffic and attention but don't directly cost money'.

Fishkin, Rand and Thomas Høgenhaven

Although there are lots of complex definitions of the term 'inbound marketing' out there, I believe the version above defines it best. If you have Facebook you'll see the latest trend of entrepreneurs developing "passive income", inbound marketing is pretty similar in that you can develop a strategy that delivers a passive way to generate new customers.

Unlike the passive income business models, I'm not saying you don't need to make an effort to generate customers. To do it properly you need to invest time and effort into researching your customers problems and producing content to help them solve them. If you get content and inbound marketing right and really align your strategy with your customers wants and needs, you could be onto a winner with a flow of consistent leads and sales for your business whilst adding value to your audience.

CHAPTER 17
Become famous for the right reasons

Successful startups and brands in the 2020s will have transparency and authenticity at the helm. We only have to look at the meteoric rise of influencer marketing in recent years to see how personal branding is essential to brand success. Huge marketing success stories like GymShark are fronted by people like Ben Francis. The Forbes 30 under 30 is a list full of inspirational leaders doing their bit for business and the world.

You need to front your brand and become the face of your organisation.

Become the person people look to for guidance. Building your own personal brand is vital and you need to get started today as it won't happen overnight. To be considered an expert and go to in an industry you need to do your time. You can't just post a few social posts and expect everyone to treat your word as gospel.

Create your own personal brand

You and your employees are the best advocates for your brand, you're knowledgeable about your industry, audience and brand. Who better to be the spokesperson for and human face of your brand?

A worry some people have when you talk about creating your own personal brand is a lack of presenting skills or confidence. No matter what your personality or specific skill set, there is a method for you to create your own personal brand. If you prefer writing you can use social media and blogging, or if you have have great public speaking skills then video might be the ideal platform for you to amplify your message.

But before you jump in and start shouting from the rooftops, just like your approach to your organisation's brand, you need a strategy. Don't waste time spinning your wheels, get focused on what personal brand building strategies are going to have the biggest impact. Start by writing a list of topics your audience might find helpful, tools like Moz Keyword Explorer and BuzzSumo could help you here to identify keywords and topics your audience are already searching for. Now you have an idea of what topics you're going to talk about it's a good idea to decide what format would best serve your audience and which fits best with your existing strengths, this will guide where you're going to publish your thought leadership content.

Write a list of content types you could use, it could include video, podcast, PDF guides to infographics, courses and webinars. Once you've decided on the type of content, the medium for sharing is important, different messages and content types work better on different platforms. You could use your own website, podcast directories, other blogs, social media, YouTube and question sites like Quora to share your content.

The most important thing here is to create a consistent content strategy for your personal brand. Plan your content ahead and post regularly, there's nothing worse than going to a blog and seeing the last post is over a year old, the same goes for your YouTube channel. Commit to a sensible posting schedule you know you can keep up with and post regularly to add value to your audience.

The beauty of personal brand building is it's primarily free, besides the time spent writing or recording your content or investment made working with a designer to produce content. Personal brand building can be as inexpensive as you want it to be.

Tools like writing blogs, posting on LinkedIn and recording videos for YouTube are free and effective in building a personal brand. LinkedIn is especially great for connecting with like minded people in your industry and beyond, posting regularly up to four times a week keeps you at the top of the mind and helps build your brand as an expert in your field. The key with any brand building activity is to use your platform to add value. Don't use your blogs or videos to self promote, create shareable content that gets your audience thinking.

Quality over regularity

For personal brand building to work, you should focus on quality content delivered consistently. Building a personal brand isn't a short term fix so you need to commit to delivering real value with your content over a long time. In the last chapter I mentioned being good at one thing, the same applies to personal branding. Start by creating one or two content types, this could be anything from blogs to videos and post them out on one or two content mediums. Test the reaction to your content, once you know you have one content type and medium nailed, try adding in new types to reach other segments of your audience.

Rushing content and overcommitting to building your personal brand can result in a haphazard approach, creating a personal brand image of a lazy, sporadic marketer - something not many of us would like to be branded as. Focus on quality over regularity.

Be visible or be forgotten

Just like brands you need to be visible to your audience too, if you're shrinking back into the background and letting your brand do the talking, you're missing out on a huge opportunity. The good news? It's not too difficult to get noticed. By posting on your own site and social networks you can reach your audience pretty easily. But if you want to be more visible, you need to be looking outside of the channels you control.

Working on getting into other publications should be a priority by working on digital PR outreach. Reach out to popular podcasts or blogs in your industry to ask how you could get featured or be interviewed. Remember they probably get lots of requests like this everyday so stand out and be specific about what you could offer. If you're reaching out to blogs, pitch a specific blog content idea. If it's for a podcast, listen to some episodes and find themes they talk about

- demonstrate your unique knowledge on one of the subjects and ask if they would be interested in interviewing you.

Public speaking can be pretty daunting but speaking at events and meetups can be a great way to become more confident while also growing your network and influence. If you're not quite ready to try public speaking, even attending local entrepreneurship and business events can help you build your network and become more visible in your space. Meeting others helps you build a base of potential partners to work with too, as you open yourself up to joint ventures and other opportunities like guest blogging, partnerships, and customer referrals.

By working to make yourself more visible in your industry you're able to build authority and credibility. You're not only serving your audience by providing value, you're also serving your organisation by becoming it's biggest ambassador.

Start now

There has never been a better time to be in business. Anyone can build an audience online if they have the right message. This does have a downside though as, depending on your business, someone could go into direct competition with you tomorrow. The good news though is that if you've followed the first two sections of this book you've got your audience and message nailed. Now you just need to amplify that message to reach as much of your audience as possible. By having a strong personal brand you can build a powerful voice in your sector, one that people look to for advice or expertise, one that is trusted and loved by your audience.

Planning and producing content to build your authority takes time. Building a personal brand doesn't happen overnight, but with more and more people seeing the benefit of building their own personal profile to expand their opportunities, you need to get started now. Use your voice to amplify your message and grow your brand.

Work with influencers

Chances are there are already people who have authority in your space, who've already done the hard work to build trust and influence. Gain trust faster by aligning yourself with them. Partnering with others is a simple strategy. Find people or brands who are established in your sector and work with them to add further value to your audience. You could partner with other organisations to run join marketing campaigns and ventures or work with influencers to help promote your products and services to their audience.

Influencer marketing works best in B2C or direct to consumer brand relationships, by aligning yourself with a trusted source you're able to increase the response from your marketing as well as winning more attention. If you're working with influencers it's important that there is an alignment in values and audience. So focus on building strong relationships with a handful of individuals who have an engaged niche audience rather than working on a transactional basis offering money for individual posts from influencers with millions of followers. You could even offer a revenue generation share to ensure the influencers you're working with are fully on board with what you're trying to achieve, removing some of the problems associated with working on a purely transactional basis.

The power of a small engaged audience

Stop aiming big and focus on a smaller audience who you can serve successfully. Instead of trying to build a large, generic following, shift your focus and energies to serving a very specific niche. Define your audience and build a community for them to thrive. By serving a defined audience you're able to focus your message so it is amplified and impactful, you build a community of people who interact and share ideas and you are rewarded with loyalty.

A few simple ideas exist to help you build communities. Facebook Groups are a good way to allow your audience to interact with you and each other. Create a place for your audience to come together and find the support they need, whether it's a group for sharing product tips and problems or just for a chat. I've talked about the power of events previously in this book but hosting events for your audience is another great way to really get to know your clients and customers. Retreats, meetups, panel discussions and dinners help you to build personal connections with each person who attends, growing your personal brand awareness and trust.

Invest in building relationships with your defined audience to spark conversations and impactful discussions. When your audience is engaged in the community you've created, the relationship moves away from being transactional to more emotional and automatic. Engaged customers are more profitable, more willing to give valuable feedback and more able to amplify your brand to new levels.

Be famous for the right reasons

We all love a bit of rubbish TV from time to time and I know I'm guilty of watching Love Island so I'm not going to launch into an attack on reality celebrities. I'll let Piers Morgan do that. But it does get you thinking. Do we place too much emphasis on celebrity and fame? Do we look carefully enough at the people we place in the spotlight? Do we put them under the microscope before we allow them to influence culture and people?

Entrepreneurs have become the new reality stars. They're placed on a pedestal. Sometimes rightfully so. But just because you've started a business, it doesn't make you a God. We should judge people by their actions, their behaviours and the change they make rather than the amount of PR stories and interviews they do. You will be remembered not only for the change you make, but the way you behave and treat others. The difference and impact you have on others and the people around you and the way that you inspire them.

What change do you want to make?

What do you want to be remembered for?

Recent stories of entrepreneurs and business owners acting in ways they shouldn't has led to the uncovering of a lot of less than ethical behaviour in business. Be remembered for the right reasons, be famous to your audience for the good you do. Amplify your message with your behaviour and actions.

Become brand led

Most industries still haven't grasped the simple concept that customers don't really care about them. They don't want to hear organisations endlessly talk about themselves, they want to be a part of the conversation where they're the centre of a brand's marketing. Successful brands use marketing to help their audience understand themselves and their needs better, they help customers learn more about their motivations and fears. The best marketing campaigns are thought provoking and ask questions of your audience.

An example of brand led versus branded companies can be seen in Airbnb and Hilton. While one is promoting an aspirational product and using tired marketing tactics to sell, the other has created a whole new segment and changed the way their audience thinks about travel.

You don't see Airbnb talking about staying in a room. You see them talking about what that room and experience allows the customer to do. Explore more, see more, do more. Their marketing pushes the idea that a room is more than a commodity. It gets the customer excited and uses emotion to create a connection and need in their mind. Move away from product led marketing to lifestyle marketing. Make your audience think, dream and ask important questions about who they are and what they want.

Don't be the best

Don't market yourself as the best, the cheapest or the fastest. Someone can always come along and knock you off your perch. Instead market your differences. Stand out and use those differences to reach your audience. Marketing focused around product benefits and price distinctions is losing its effectiveness because of the sheer number of competitors in each industry.

Instead, focus on creating a distinct point of difference in your audience's mind with your marketing.

Beyoncé and David Bowie

What do Beyonce and David Bowie have to do with marketing?

Quite a lot actually, they both created an unstoppable worldwide brand through constant reinvention. They experimented with their craft and remained fluid in their direction of travel. Stars like Bowie push their genres, they're not bound by norms and expectations of the market: they adapt and experiment to help expand their audience and fan base.

Beyoncé didn't push her political purpose straight away, it took two decades of preparation, improvement   and dedication to build the platform she stands on today. She may be one of the hardest working entertainers of our time but her talents have developed far beyond the Single Ladies video, she has worked hard to develop a brand that allows her a voice. A voice she uses to raise awareness of burning issues like the gender and racial inequalities that exist in our society. She built her BeyHive to amplify her voice and cause. Beyonce is bigger than Beyonce now, she is a symbol of black culture and a voice for feminism. The foundations she has built over the years through her own music, marketing and partnerships has allowed her to use her voice for good

You have the opportunity to do the same. Push the boundaries of your industry. Be brave with your marketing, speak directly to your audience and don't be afraid to alienate some and stand for causes that aren't "mainstream" enough for your competitors to talk about in their marketing.

Just like Beyoncé you need to dedicate yourself to serving your audience to enable you to build a strong platform to speak your purpose.

Sustainability, ethics and culture aren't marketing tricks

Your purpose is your driving force; it needs to be unique and stand the test of time. In a world of corporate greenwashing and sustainability band wagons, you need to stand out. Simply saying you're a sustainable and ethical brand isn't enough. Your customers can see through greenwashing and demand real action on the causes you stand for.

Sustainability, ethics and a strong culture won't be "a nice to have" in five years time: they won't be effective marketing campaign topics. They will be a given. Be on the right side of the argument and build the foundations of a sustainable and ethical brand from day one. You can't amplify your message with marketing if you don't get the basics right, your empowered audience have all the tools they need to identify BS. Don't use sustainability as a marketing trick, treat it as a must have to build a brand and be famous for the right reasons.

Key Person of Influence

In his book Key Person of Influence, Daniel Priestley talks about the need for different types of people within a business. One of the crucial team members is the Key Person of Influence (KPI). They hold the key to unlocking awareness and trust amongst your target customers and prospects. They're the go-to voice on niche topics in their industry, they're well known and liked by many.

This whole chapter has been, amongst other things, about becoming your own KPI. Greta Thunberg and David Attenburgh didn't become key people in the climate change movement by accident; they placed themselves in the argument; they got involved, spoke out and provided a voice for their audience. They amplified the message of their audience and used their platform as a Key Person of Influence to do more good.

They produce written content, take part in interviews, post videos and tell stories. You can do the same by following the principles in this book. Don't stand around and wait for the Greta of your cause; become the Key Person of Influence in your space:

Serve and lead

The power of amplification is best seen through serving. By serving your audience over time you're amplifying the effect of your message, as you reach and serve more of your audience they become true fans of your brand. You create an army of allies, people who live for your brand. They want you brand to succeed as much as you do so they actively promote on your behalf and share their positive experiences.

Marketing is often treated as something mystical, where only the best in the industry can deliver sustainable growth to business and charity. While lots of organisations find marketing difficult, when you really understand the basics of marketing and become a leader who serves and puts their audience first, marketing becomes much less of a mystery.

Don't be a take take take marketer or entrepreneur. Be a leader who serves.

CHAPTER 18
Start serving your audience

The time is now for you to thrive. Purpose driven marketing is now mainstream and you can ride the wave by serving your own niche to deliver value. Define your purpose, communicate your message and amplify it to reach your audience.

Define your brand

Without a clear defined reason for existing your brand is another me too brand to get lost in the sea of brands losing out to more successful brands with a clearly defined audience to serve. A laser focused brand strategy and definition of who your audience is and what they care about is the bloodline of your brand.

Research is vital and time spent researching your market and audience is some of the best time you will ever invest when growing a brand. By immersing yourself in the sector, you can better understand the issues your audience is facing to better meet and exceed the needs of your customers.

The end goal of the Define stage of your brand journey is to occupy a clearly defined place in the heads and hearts of your audience. When you get branding right, you build strong emotional relationships with people who will help you grow and develop.

Be brave. Choose a niche audience and develop a brand that serves their needs. Your less focused competition will flit between customers, never building loyalty or strong foundations for their brand. The world needs you to take a stand and create a brand based around real action, unique values and a purpose. Serve your audience and deliver the impact they want you to deliver.

Communicate with your audience

You've chosen your audience. You've defined your reasons for existing and pledged to a better way of marketing by serving their needs, now what?

You need to take a consistent approach to your communications strategy. You need to build a culture of honest and authentic communication in your organisation, one where your customer takes centre stage and is at the forefront of decisions. If you're running an existing brand you can take the opportunity to map out all of your existing communications across digital and offline channels and make sure they're consistent. By taking a holistic approach to visual communication auditing, you can identify weak documents and strong, impactful communications that can be used to improve your overall communication strategy. Templating your communications has given you a consistent approach to developing your visual communications from templated posters to social posts.

A lack of consistency in your communications results in a confused audience. Confused audiences don't buy and don't have the tools they need to share your message far and wide with people who fit your definition of ideal customers. Communicating your message effectively using the Communicate stage of the brand building process is vital to the success of your brand.

Amplify your message

You've defined your audience, you have templates and documents communicating your message effectively. It's time to amplify your message with marketing. Taking a continuous marketing improvement approach, you can develop a well oiled marketing machine that uses learning to iterate and deliver better marketing results.

You've added storytelling and content marketing to your armoury of marketing strategies and you're using an ethical approach to marketing. You will use your position responsibly to reach your audience ethically always considering how your actions as a marketer or entrepreneur affect others and the planet.

When you follow the three stage process for marketing success, by defining who you're going to serve, creating a strategy to communicate consistently with your audience and amplifying your message by using marketing to support, inspire and educate people to take action, you create an unstoppable brand built on strong ethical foundations ready to take on the world and make the change you want to deliver as an entrepreneur and marketer.

It's your time to go ahead and serve your audience, there has never been a better time to serve. Don't sit around waiting for someone else to take up the role of leader, you have the skills and now the process to build a brand with impact.

Go ahead.

Make the change you want to make in the world.

Appendix One
Patagonia: The power of purpose

"We're in business to save the planet"

The mission statement of outdoor apparel company Patagonia is pretty bold. Founder of the brand, Yvon Chouinard wanted to build an organisation for people who shared his passion for exploring and protecting nature. Since the 70s when the business was founded Patagonia has become an aspirational clothing brand for a loyal fan base. With increasing mainstream concern for the environment the brand is going from strength to strength. An example of how serving an audience over a sustained period of time rewards the brand with sustainable growth.

In a world of fast fashion, Patagonia has been pushing the agenda for a more sustainable approach to clothing and retail for decades. They focus on producing long lasting garments and were amongst the first championing recycling used garments with WornWear, their "program that keeps gear in action longer."

The best example of a purpose driven brand?

Patagonia is perhaps the best example of standing for something that leads to business success. With many companies treating sustainability and ethics as a CSR issue, Patagonia has embedded its purpose at its core and everything the business does is driven by it.

Under CEO Rose Marcario the brand has doubled down on the issues important to the brand. In a world of Trump and Brexit it would be easy for brands to cave to populist views, but instead the brand has stuck to its message and gone further with public statements against the president's policies that have actually grown sales.

By truly understanding their audience and what's important to them they stand at the edges of their industry ready to take a stand against even the most powerful people to serve their audience.

By having a purpose, following through on its core values and actively contributing to the environmental conversation they have positioned themselves as the aspirational clothing brand for people who care about the world they live in.

1% for the planet

Consumers are demanding more of the brands they buy from and Patagonia has been leading the way on ethical fashion for a while. They are championed for their commitment to the planet with all of their cotton certified organic and a large proportion of their materials being made from recycled fabrics.

Their commitment to 1% For The Planet started in 1986 when founder Yvon Chouinard committed to giving 1% of sales revenue to the "preservation and restoration of the natural environment." Since then the company has embarked on two notable Black Friday campaigns, the first in 2011 when Patagonia printed a full-page ad in The New York Times encouraging customers to not buy its products.

More recently in 2016 when the company gave 100% of Black Friday sales to grassroots environmental organisations it raised $10 million in revenue and gained 24,000 new customers in one day.

It's hard to quantify the positive effects their environmental issues have on sales but it's easy to see how 24,000 new customers can add to the long term sales success of the company.

Caring for people

One of the criticisms made against fast fashion retailers is that of poor labour conditions.

Patagonia received the second highest rating in the 2017 Ethical Fashion Report, which takes into consideration payment of a living wage and worker empowerment. They are transparent about who they work with and publicly lists suppliers - something fashion retailers often prefer to hide.

They have taken steps to build a sustainable supply chain that works for everyone involved, not just the shareholders.

Transparency and quick responses to sustainability concerns

One of the words most often used to describe Patagonia is transparent.

Whenever the company has been caught short on its own commitment to animal welfare or workers' rights it has been quick to respond and take action. When its use of bird feathers in products was questioned it was quick to rectify the issue and work with Four Paws and other brands like The North Face to commit to only using down produced without animal suffering.

Patagonia: A blueprint for business?

Without being too fangirly here, Patagonia has been leading the way on how to do business for years and more brands need to take note.

What can we learn from Patagonia and the three key elements of their success?

Sustainability: Businesses can't continue taking. Consumers are demanding more and sustainability is something climbing to the top of a lot of people's lists of values. Brands who don't look at the impact they're having on the planet will find themselves left behind as customers leave them in favour of more sustainable brands that align with their world view.

Transparency: Patagonia hasn't got a perfect track record but the difference is they respond quickly and effectively. When they're called out for something (having known about it or not) they take big action to rectify the issue. They pride themselves on being open - something consumers love and buy into.

Standing for something and serving people who care about it: By having a purpose at its core the brand has been able to attract and serve customers and employees who are passionate about the same issues. Innovative marketing wins have been suggested by employees who have bought into the brand's mission. It's reported the 2016 Black Friday 100% For The Planet Campaign was signed off by the CEO within 30 minutes in a text message! By standing for something Patagonia has been able to attract the right team consistently over many, many years.

Patagonia embedded themselves in the sustainability conversation, their consistency in serving their audience with their initiatives, products and messaging has led them to have a dedicated tribe of people who live the brand. An example for us all to follow.

Appendix Two
The Serve Manifesto

A pledge to a better way of marketing.

The manifesto has some of the rules I think marketers should follow to move towards value driven marketing and become the marketer you and your audience deserves.

1. I will make the change I seek to make.

2. I will serve my audience, even when it seems like nobody else is listening.

3. I will stick with my cause and not flit to the latest shiny thing.

4. I will not overpromise and underdeliver.

5. I will deliver real value to my audience.

6. I will always think carefully about how the decisions I make in business can affect others and the environment.

7. I will behave in a way that inspires others.

Appendix Three
Further reading list

No idea is 100% original, ideas are shaped by our influences and learnings.

As a keen reader, I've read tonnes of inspiring content and thought provoking books which have helped shape my thinking, values and beliefs. Here are just some of the books that have helped shape my ideas and better manage my day which has allowed me to write this book and build the confidence needed to finish it.

Oversubscribed, Daniel Priestley

Key Person of Influence, Daniel Priestley

Atomic Habits, James Clear

This Is Marketing, Seth Godin

Blue Ocean Strategy, Renée Mauborgne and W. Chan Kim

Branding: In Five and a Half Steps, Michael A. Johnson

The Compound Effect, Darren Hardy

From Impossible to Inevitable, Aaron Ross and Jason Lemkin

Printed in Great Britain
by Amazon

76248884R00102